THE PSYCHIC ABILITIES OF BEING AN EMPATH

A PRACTICAL GUIDE TO SETTING BOUNDARIES
WITHOUT FEELING GUILTY, PROTECTING
YOURSELF, AND INCREASING YOUR SELF-
ESTEEM SO YOU CAN TAKE CONTROL BACK
OVER YOUR LIFE

S.C. Rowse

.

CONTENTS

INTRODUCTION

Being an empath is a gift. But empaths can feel overwhelmed by painful emotions. I found I could mitigate the pain with specific strategies which I will share with you in this book. I learned that setting boundaries was vital to my personal and emotional development. By learning to protect myself without feeling guilty, I was able to grow into the person I am today. These days I am a hypnotherapist, and it brings me joy to help people grow even when others try to bring them down. The knowledge I acquired changed my life, and I've devoted myself to spreading that wisdom because I know it can also help others change their lives as well.

Being an empath can take a toll on your emotional well-being. You might wonder if your sensitivity to suffering is hiding your true potential. You might find yourself repeatedly emotionally abused by various people without knowing how to stop it and with only the vaguest idea of why it happens. Perhaps you are even being physically ill-treated because of your empathy. Your present situation causes you pain, and it's because you are "too sensitive." As a result, you go through life mired in anxiety, depression, and the feeling that you're not good enough. Even attempts to resolve your problems overwhelm you with negative energy, leaving you drained and irritable and lamenting your inability to say no and cope with what you have undertaken to do.

Nevertheless, you know that your empathic abilities are ultimately a gift, just as I do. You want to use them to their fullest potential, which means growing and healing from your traumas. Your attempts to solve your problems by yourself are evidence of your strong will, and there are ways to use that energy to move forward and hone your empathic skills. If you put in the effort without going beyond your limits, you may even be able to use your abilities to heal others.

Before you commit to helping anyone else, however, you must help yourself. Imagine going through life without feeling constantly overwhelmed and feeling guilty for setting boundaries. The joy you will experience without this negative energy will speak for itself. More than just feeling better, you will make real progress in life. Unfettered by the restrictions of guilt and anxiety, you will feel motivated to achieve your goals. I will give you the tools to take these steps, and you will get the strength to heal your wounds and move forward.

The tools mentioned consist of exercises and practices that describe methods for setting boundaries and healing from your traumas. You will also learn to use self-hypnosis together with your empathic gifts to heal yourself and others. You may not understand all these tools in the first few chapters. It is essential to understand empathy and its corresponding abilities first, but you will have the necessary tools to move onward when you do.

When people like us struggle with the pitfalls of our empathic tendencies, we need someone who understands and is dedicated to solving our problems. Even if I weren't as involved with the empath lifestyle as I am, I would still endeavor to understand your experiences and help you find solutions to what is troubling you. It may sound overly simplistic, but it's true: I would much rather help the people around me find happiness than let them languish in pain. As you read this book, I want you to know that I am here for you, and that is what this book is for.

Of course, this book isn't about me, my presence, or my experiences. This book is about you, helping you to learn about yourself and to give you what you need to be your best self. Yes, that's a lot of emphasis on you, but that's how it should be. The best place to start on your empathic journey is to understand what an empath is at their core and what you are at your core. From here, we will jump right into the definition of an empath and learn about the specific problems faced by empaths. In the first chapter, we will focus on the basics. Don't fret about how to start mending yourself just yet. You need to know what you're working with first. Stay calm, form a strong foundation, and take your first steps.

1

WHAT DOES IT REALLY MEAN TO BE AN EMPATH?

WHAT IS A TRUE EMPATH?

It would be best to build the foundation of your understanding with a solid definition of what an empath is. A peek into popular definitions of the term allows one to glean a good composite of what an empath should be (certain derogatory definitions aside). For our purposes, we'll define an empath as:

"A person who experiences and understands the mental and emotional states of others on a deep level, which also allows them to sense the energies others give out."

In this case, a deep level refers to an understanding so strong that an empath can embody and process another person's emotions. Incorporating a person's feelings can be an almost literal experience, with the other person's emotions becoming absorbed and affecting your body in a way that is deeply felt.

TYPES OF EMPATHS

There are multiple types of empaths as well as degrees of empathic ability.

Emotional Empaths – you feel the emotions of those around you as your own.

Medical Empaths – or "Medical Intuitive" – you are aware or can feel another's physical pain and illnesses even in those far from your present location.

Nature Empaths–you know or bring in the feelings of things and animals in the natural world – plants, trees, and animals.

Intellectual Empath or Claircognizant Empath–you know what another person is like and can emulate them.

Spiritual Empaths – you can feel the true essence of people, places, and other beings, both present and past.

SKILLS AND PERSONALITIES

A few commonalities among these different categories of empaths allow them to exist under one umbrella term. A strong intuition is one such trait, sometimes to the point of telepathy or clairvoyance. However, clairvoyance is not a requirement for being an empath.

All empathic types typically absorb the feelings of others. However, emotional empaths are particularly susceptible. They must consciously shed the emotions they have absorbed from everyone around them or become emotionally exhausted. This exhaustion can make empaths even more vulnerable to being manipulated and overwhelmed.

The following fact may be evident to us, but it merits emphasizing on the record: EMPATHS ARE REAL. We viscerally feel not only our own emotions but those of others. This ability allows us to help others process their feelings, perhaps by assisting them in finding the words for what they are feeling. But, of course, you cannot properly help others until you have helped yourself. In general, empaths struggle with caring for themselves. In fact, different types of empaths have many problems in common. We will address these difficulties and give you tools to cope with them later in the book; however, it is essential to identify them now. You may not even be aware that what you are experiencing is a problem, let alone an "empath problem," and that's why it's time to outline some of them.

EIGHT PROBLEMS ONLY EMPATHS WILL UNDERSTAND

Below we have highlighted eight of the most common "empath problems." There are others, of course, so please do your research and take care of yourself.

Empaths have real difficulty disconnecting from others' emotions

The first one is that the emotions of others can immediately alter your own emotional state, regardless of what has happened to you. Even if you've had a wonderful day, if someone close to you comes home feeling less than stellar, your emotions immediately shift to match theirs. Empaths have difficulty disconnecting others' emotions from their own and often need to expend extra energy and vigilance to keep their feelings separate.

Emotional fatigue

Emotional fatigue is a significant problem for empaths due to the focus required to process their emotions, both positive and negative, as well as those of the people around them. Therefore, empaths must practice regular self-care to mitigate and prevent exhaustion. Remember, there is no need to worry about how to do this at this stage. You only need to know that it is something that you have to actively practice in your empath lifestyle.

Not being able to turn off that compassion

Your compassion will often feel like a burden. People will tell you that you're too sensitive or care too much about minor things, and you will be left wondering why they don't care more. Not being able to turn off that compassion easily can make you feel like you're suffering more than anyone around you. Because that suffering is "abnormal," you're solely responsible for alleviating it in both yourself and others. Of course, after a certain point, others must help themselves, and you will learn when and how to set boundaries and make it clear that you cannot help people at the cost of your health.

Empaths need alone time to heal their own emotions; however, complete isolation is not healthy

Balancing alone time with fostering healthy relationships is yet another challenge that empaths face. There is some overlap between empaths and introverts, though they aren't quite the same. While empaths do need alone time to heal their own emotions and let go of what they've collected from others, complete isolation is rarely, if ever, a healthy option. Some empaths find small gatherings in quieter places like coffee shops to be a reasonable compromise in terms of interaction and atmosphere. On that note, other people may not understand your need for alone time, and you may find yourself engaged in lengthy discussions with your more sociable counterparts as to why you need time to rest and clear your head. You may need to explain that you struggle with transitions, making it hard to go from quiet places to loud ones and vice versa.

Anxiety and depression

Struggles with mental health, particularly anxiety and

depression, are common among some but not all empaths. Their innate sensitivity to emotions can amplify "small" emotions into full-on attacks of self-doubt and stress. Rejection, particularly when paired with anger or disappointment, can be devastating for empaths as they process their own hurt and the scorn of the person who rejected them. The two-hit combination of emotions can result in empaths taking on the physical aspects of others' conditions on top of their own, resulting in significant pain. Emotional shocks stack up, making self-care paramount for any empath, however tricky it may be at the time.

Vulnerability to taking on others' emotions and bringing oneself down

As one might expect, an empath is highly attuned and sensitive to other people's energy, making it easy for them to perceive when someone is troubled. While it helps you discern who needs help, it makes you vulnerable to taking on their emotions and bringing yourself down. Related to that tendency is a susceptibility to people who take advantage of an empath's compassion. While your intuition may point to a person not being quite on the level, no radar is always perfect, and sometimes narcissists and toxic people will get past your defenses. This aspect of being an empath is yet another reason boundaries are so important. It is also essential to take careful stock of your interactions with others.

A tendency to magnify the emotions in and around them

Because an empath tends to magnify the emotions in and around them, there are no "small" things. Empaths care about almost everything, and even "minor" insults or slights can worry them for days. Someone else may ask why they can't just "get over it" and "move on." Of course, it isn't that simple for empaths. If it was, why would there be so much focus on releasing the collected emotions of others?

Not being able to tell which emotions are genuinely yours

It is important to note that an emotional source need not be direct or nearby to wreak havoc on an empath. Violent scenes on TV or in the news can leave you wondering how anyone can move on with their day after watching something like that. That concept leads us to a final common empath problem: not being able to tell which emotions are truly yours, which are absorbed from people around you, or from even further afield. The tangle of feelings can make decisions difficult. Keeping track of where everything came from can be exhausting in itself. It isn't always possible to release the collected emotions before making decisions, but at least try to analyze them.

DARK EMPATHS: DEFINITION AND KEY TRAITS

Now that we have addressed common problems among empaths, we can turn our focus to some rarer ones. A phenomenon known as "dark empaths" exists among a small percentage of the population. These empaths combine apparently dark and cold outward personality traits with the kindness and compassion associated with typical empaths. Some are good people under their more concerning traits, but others use their understanding of other people to manipulate them. The meaning of the "dark" classification and the traits that make it so come from a set of personality constructs called the dark triad. These three traits are narcissism (self-centeredness), Machiavellianism (deception and cold personality), and psychopathy (dissociation from others and reality).

The brighter side of dark empathy creates people like the media's famous anti-heroes, mysterious and morally gray characters with beautiful hearts. Dark empaths express high extroversion (rare among any type of empath), openness, and willingness to express their emotions to others. Neurotic traits may also be part of the package, indicating mood swings, anxiety, and emotional pain. Dark empaths enjoy connecting with people and being leaders, with their empathy tempering the need for power and making their leadership more humane. Still, they may have a particular sort of vulnerable narcissism. They understand the hurts of others but feel any hurts directed at them very keenly.

Still, there may be a reason to flinch at hearing that

dark empaths are partly narcissistic. Those deemed psychopaths may not be utterly devoid of empathy, and empathy is not necessarily related to aggression. A dark empath may demonstrate some aggression, mostly indirect (think piercing humor or guilt-tripping), but may also display high sociability and amiability. All the same, they can weaponize their empathy. We usually think of affective empathy in these cases, i.e., sharing someone's feelings on an emotional level.

However, cognitive empathy is a type of empathy where a person takes a more intellectual approach when observing another person's situation. People high in psychopathy strive to learn "correct" behaviors to mimic empathy, but studies have demonstrated that their brains don't quite light up when imagining the pain of others. This sort of simulated empathy isn't genuine empathy, and it may be used to manipulate you or otherwise profit at your expense.

Furthering the notion that cognitive empathy can be dangerous is the existence of dissonant components like schadenfreude and bona fide sadism. Specific questions on the Affective and Cognitive Measure of Empathy test ask about joy from making others feel stupid, wanting to hurt others if you could get away with it, and pleasure in watching others get angry. This sort of effective dissonance has quite strong associations with aggressive behavior. A dark empath may also exhibit skewed expressions of empathy that favor those similar to the empath and smaller groups. However, it is worth noting that anyone can be vulnerable to this effect. Empathy can skew decision-making processes in anyone and polarize feelings to dangerous extents.

Having covered the common and rare traits of empaths, it may help to zoom out and lead into the more practical aspects of being an empath, namely pointing out common triggers and the surface-level tricks to dealing with them. You may not be satisfied with the simplified solutions, but I assure you that we will go more in depth after covering all the basics of being an empath. It would not do to have you learn the complete exercises when you can't directly recall what they apply to.

TRIGGERS FOR EMOTIONAL TRAUMA

There are at least seven possible triggers of emotional trauma for empaths:

Feeling the pain of others, while a constant and consistent hazard for all empaths, can serve as a trigger for deep trauma if prolonged and profound enough. The mere act of shouldering everyone's burdens can cause a *tremendous amount of energy drain*, but doing it for too long with no boundaries or rest can cause severe damage to an empath's mental health. So naturally, setting said boundaries and resting when feeling overwhelmed are vital tools to prevent this.

A less obvious trigger but still one that is present nonetheless is the feeling of *being misunderstood*. Since it is so difficult to parse both your emotions and those of others, people may not understand your way of processing your feelings, and the longer you go believing no one understands you, the more ingrained the feeling can become. A simple solution is to know the value of your gift. Ultimately, only you need to understand yourself, and your ability to understand others on such a deep level is just a bonus that will empower you to help others.

Along these lines, yet not entirely the same is *feeling unvalued*. It is one thing to be wanted and another to be considered worthy in someone's eyes. Feeling worthless can cause empaths to experience downward spirals where they cannot see their own worth. While feeling appreciated by others is a major boon for empaths, they first need to value themselves. You cannot rely on others for validation. It may help to think of the nature of your gift: You have the ability to help others now and in the future. Feeling unloved ties all those negative feelings together, as low self-esteem can make an empath feel unloved from the start. It helps to open your mind and realize that someone out there loves you, even if that person is yourself.

Acceptance is a powerful energy source for an empath, but *rejection* exists, and it hits empaths particularly hard. When not everyone accepts you as you are or strangers reject you, it becomes easy to forget simple concepts. Your existing relationships are more important than those with strangers, and a stranger's acceptance or rejection of you doesn't always matter. Focus on what you have instead of what you don't have. This will bolster your will to keep going and keep trying.

However, there is a flip side to all the missing feelings as triggers. Sometimes, being wanted can be a trigger. On the one hand, being *liked by the wrong people* for the wrong purposes can set you off, as can being loved by too many people. On the other hand, realizing a toxic person is manipulating you and having to cut them off can be as painful as receiving their attention, and it can certainly leave their mark for a long time to come. It is essential to know what is best for you in the long run and that you can withstand the pain if it brings you peace. As for being *wanted by too many people,* the overwhelming quantity and quality of people's requests can weigh an empath down until they burn out. The key to managing everyone's wants, including your own, is to set boundaries. It's a vital concept, and that's why it recurs so often.

EXTROVERTED EMPATH

There is one more item to cover when discussing empaths: the rare case of the extroverted empath. As stated earlier, there is some overlap between introverts and empaths, with both requiring space to focus on themselves and both favoring smaller groups over larger ones. All the same, an empath needs some interaction for the sake of their emotional health. The extension of this concept is the extroverted empath, an empath who actively seeks out and enjoys the energies and interactions of others.

An account from one such extroverted empath points out the inherent paradox of extroverted empaths: the extroverted side thrives around people. In contrast, the empath side struggles being bombarded with all those people's energy. Empaths highlight the compromise of engaging with smaller and more familiar groups without taking in too much potentially overwhelming energy. Extroverted empaths also have their own tools for processing social interactions, although some are the same as those used by regular empaths. These include mindfulness (in the sense of awareness of your senses), taking breaks, and making sure to have time completely for themselves, but we're going to delve into those in more detail later. An extroverted empath is extremely rare. In a recent study, one to two percent of the population consisted of empaths, while anywhere from fifty to seventy-four percent of the entire population may be extroverted. Given how empaths take in the energy of people around them and experience side effects from doing so, it makes sense that the small percentage of the population that consists of empaths doesn't quite lend itself to extroversion. This tendency leads to what is veritably a slice of the population being extroverted empaths, so a tiny sliver indeed. Still, it is important to mention these rarities when discussing empaths because they do exist and should be given attention like every other key concept.

CHAPTER SUMMARY

There are quite a few places on the internet and in books that help you define what an empath is and what the traits of an empath are. Having a list which you can access and compare for yourself might be helpful. A couple of the most predominant characteristics are:

Empaths are highly sensitive—they can feel the emotions of those around them.

Empaths absorb other people's emotions—they bring those feelings into themselves as their own.

Empaths are highly intuitive – they can almost instinctively know what someone is going through.

Empaths need alone time—with all those emotions flying around people all the time, they need time to be by themselves.

Empaths can become overwhelmed in intimate relationships –this makes sense as people are very involved in each other's feelings in intimate relationships.

Empaths become targets for energy vampires – as with most things, there will always be those people wanting to take advantage of others.

Empaths love animals and nature – they seem in tune with nature and animals, love to garden, and feel the earth beneath their feet.

Empaths have highly tuned senses – through years of practice mostly born of necessity, they have developed their primary senses as well–smell, touch, etc.

Empaths have huge hearts but sometimes give too much –it is in their nature to share more of themselves.

Empaths read people's emotions – whether through necessity and/or practice, they can read the emotions emanating from those around them.

Empaths have unpredictable mood swings –they need a lot of practice to separate their emotions from other people's feelings.

Empaths are free spirits –this is a coping mechanism as it helps empaths go off alone and recharge their energy and feelings of well-being.

Empaths are problem solvers –they want to be to "fix" things and keep coming up with different ways to solve whatever problem is currently being dealt with.

Empaths are creative –this is a natural extension of their personalities. It allows the brain to get rid of all of these emotional states in a productive manner.

Empaths are sometimes too forgiving – Sadly, empaths all hope that if given enough chances, a person will change.

Empaths discover lies and deceptions astonishingly quickly— empaths can spot the lie; however, it doesn't mean they deal with it effectively.

Empaths have an innate desire to better the world –YES! If only people would listen and feel what empaths feel, the world would be a better place.

Empaths dislike selfish, dull, and mean people – life is much too short to be around or act like these people.

Empaths are often obsessed with order and cleanliness – emotions are messy, so it is vital that the surrounding environment be as clean and ordered as possible.

Empaths suffer from chronic fatigue–with all this data coming in and out of their brains and hearts, their poor bodies just feel so tired.

Empaths dislike violence and drama –negative emotions of any kind are not good for empaths. They would rather just go away and not see or hear about these kinds of things.

Empaths might suffer from lower back problems –since most humans hold stress in their lower backs, those muscles tighten to ready our bodies for the blows that may be coming, physically or emotionally.

Empaths hate injustice –the most damaging thing is

their perceived notions about injustice. We are taught at an early age to be "fair" in all of our dealings.

Empaths are introverts, but they can be extroverts, too – there are all kinds of people in the world, so there must also be all kinds of empaths.

If you are an empath, chances are you have taken on the emotions of others on more than one occasion. To save yourself and your sanity, there are many ways to help yourself and your emotional well-being. Throughout the rest of this book, we will talk about these things and give you some tools to help develop some survival skills. Being an empath can be great at times and devastating at others, but getting to know yourself and your abilities and how to help yourself is paramount. You need to take care of you!

A couple of things to keep in mind: You are only human. You have to help yourself before you can help anyone else. Increase your knowledge about your own triggers and those of other empaths. Keep learning and taking care of yourself.

In the next chapter, we will be discussing the psychic abilities of empaths and how to determine if you are one or not, your superpowers, and which type of empath you might be.

2

WHAT IS A PSYCHIC EMPATH AND HOW TO TELL IF YOU ARE ONE

SUPERPOWERS OF AN EMPATH

Vision – You see, feel, and immerse yourself in what others cannot. Learn to use your powers for good.

Intuition – You know without being told what others are feeling, so you must learn to protect yourself while keeping yourself open to helping others.

Psychic Ability – You can sense what "our people" might be going through, whether near or far, so you can lend a hand.

Presence – Since you can feel what someone is going through, your mere "presence" can help them.

Power to Heal – Once you have mastered your ability to self-care, you can help others heal.

Creativity – Being able to sense what others around you are thinking and feeling, you can come up with unusual solutions to solve problems.

There are a couple of things you can do right now to help you begin your empathic journey:

a) Set rock-solid boundaries for yourself and the people you deal with.
b) Create and use an effective means to process and eliminate excess energy.
c) Communicate your needs in a clear and effective way.

DIFFERENCE BETWEEN BEING AN EMPATH AND A PSYCHIC EMPATH

Empaths, in general, are considered receptive and sensitive to the energy surrounding them. *On the other hand, psychic empaths can detect actual energy fields and auras around them or their surroundings, including people, animals, and plants.* I know that may not sound much of a distinction. However, the more you learn and practice your abilities, the better you will be able to differentiate between the two.

Psychic empaths, in particular, would rather be alone; they experience unstable moods, are attracted to other people's negative emotions, and feel sick and gloomy for no apparent cause. Some social situations cause enormous traumatic stress. Most empaths quickly learn how to shield themselves, expel negative energies, and focus on the most critical issues. With practice and learning, so can you.

WHAT ARE THE PSYCHIC EMPATH'S SKILLS, AND HOW TO DEVELOP THEM?

Those considered "psychic" empaths have specific skills; there are ways to develop those into really useful tools. Empathy can be a survival trait. It hones your instincts to quickly identify who needs help and who should be avoided. You can use these tools in your personal and your professional life.

Some of these skills include the ability to sense both positive and negative feelings in those around you. You can put yourself in someone else's shoes. This is always the first step in understanding their point of view and getting them to see yours. Then, together, you can begin to solve whatever problems you are currently working on. The universe can become your oyster.

Developing your particular set of skills takes time, patience, and practice. First, you have to meet and talk with various people (empaths and those who are not) to determine what works and what does not. Do not be impatient with yourself or others. It is a lifelong learning process. Instead, practice setting boundaries, experiment with dispelling excess energy through natural means (deep breathing, burning natural oils, or just walking barefoot in the warm or cool sand), and, above all else, learn to take care of yourself. Only then can you help others.

TYPES OF PSYCHIC EMPATHS

Claircognizant Empaths —have developed the ability to tell when people are lying and what should be done in most situations.

Telepathic Empaths—have the ability to understand the thinking process of humans, plants and animals.

Psychometric Empaths — can receive impressions, images, and feelings from the inanimate objects of the wearer.

Precognitive Empaths — receive emotional or physical sensations through dreams. This enables the empath to foresee future events.

Geomantic Empaths—have the skills to read the signals coming from the Earth through the soil, air, water, or even rocks. (Many animals have this ability.)

Medium Empaths — tune into the spiritual energies of people to intuit past, present, and even future events that may affect their lives using the help of beings on the non-material plane.

Reminder: While a psychic empath who has honed their gifts through years of practice may be excellent at their craft, they cannot fix every problem they encounter nor predict and mitigate every wrong.

WHAT PSYCHIC ABILITIES ARE AND WHAT THEY ARE NOT

Psychic abilities are not instinct. Instinct is innate and built within animals of all kinds and happens naturally. Instinct tells you what to do or not do. Birds returning to their nesting grounds year after year is an instinct. Being afraid of the dark and unknown is a human instinct long associated with cave dwellers. Psychic abilities start with intuition — the vague sense or feeling about something or someone. Your body and mind begin to intuit a good or bad feeling or situation that may or may not affect you or someone you know. Psychic empaths have these feelings and thoughts from people they do not even know or who may even be miles away.

CHAPTER SUMMARY

This chapter serves as a jumping-off point for those who are now beginning to commit to the "Empath Lifestyle." You have learned about the powers of an empath and the difference between a regular empath and a psychic one. It is more than a matter of degree and commitment. Some abilities need to be honed as well. Every person should naturally feel compassion for their fellow humans when faced with trying, emotional, or stressful times but empaths take on the pain of others. It is not a very comfortable way to live.

In the next chapter, you will better understand what a psychic is and is not. There are all kinds of misconceptions about empaths and their ability to be empathetic. There will also be some helpful information on how to awaken your own psychic abilities, nurture them, and use them wisely.

3

AWAKEN YOUR PSYCHIC ABILITIES

Whenever I want to learn something new, I usually try to look for reliable and "known" sources of information. There are not a lot of verifiable scientific studies we can use to help us better understand empaths and psychics and their abilities. To begin, let's look at the Psychic Definition & Meaning - Merriam-Webster:

Definition of psychic

1. 1: of or relating to the psyche: PSYCHOGENIC
2. 2: lying outside the sphere of physical science or knowledge: immaterial, moral, or spiritual in origin or force
3. 3: sensitive to nonphysical or supernatural forces and influences: marked by extraordinary or mysterious sensitivity, perception, or understanding

---

Now, right off the bat, we get the feeling that there is not going to be a lot of proven information out there. Therefore, we must rely solely on those who have experienced these things and have the courage to share their experience and their techniques for coping.

> *"There are more things in Heaven and Earth, Horatio, than are dreamt of in your philosophy."*

-William Shakespeare, Hamlet

MYTH-BUSTING

There are many myths about empaths out there, and most of them are based on the notion that empaths do not exist. Clearly, it is impossible to identify what is or is not real in this world, and just because we may not be able to understand or have not experienced things ourselves does not make them false. Empaths get sapped of energy because they are a "sponge" for other people's energy. Sometimes it is helpful to think of the properties of electricity. If you shoot too much electricity into a circuit, it will blow. Now for some of the more common myths:

Myth: All empaths are good people

I'm sorry to say this is a ridiculous thing even to think, let alone say. People are people, no matter their abilities, backgrounds, or current living conditions. There are good people, bad people, and many people who are sometimes good and sometimes bad. It is all a matter of perspective.

Myth: Empaths are always empathetic

Empaths feel the emotions of others and can choose whether or not to express "compassion a.k.a., empathy" for and about those feelings.

Myths: Empaths are attracted to egomaniacs

Empaths genuinely desire to help everyone. But unfortunately, the vibe they give off attracts those individuals who are self-absorbed and want to bask in any and everyone who will reflect their greatness back to them.

Myth: Empaths can also be narcissists

According to the psychological definitions, empaths and narcissists are at opposite ends of the emotional spectrum.

Myth: Empaths are all introverts

This is another generalization about people. Empaths may prefer to be introverted most of the time, but sometimes they want to be among people, and some even enjoy bouts of extroversion for fun and healing.

Myth: You can stop being an empath

Empathy is something you are born with, like blue eyes. You can stop using and developing your skills (usually to your detriment), but you will always be an empath.

Myth: Empaths have all been casualties of great physical and emotional pain

Intense emotional situations can make you more intuitive to protect yourself from harm. Unfortunately, empaths can become traumatized by all the energy and emotions they receive daily and must learn how to protect themselves.

AM I A PSYCHIC AND WHAT DOES IT MEAN TO MY EVERYDAY LIFE?

The previous chapter gave you a basic understanding of the kinds of powers that the empath may possess, as well as the types of empaths. Here we will go over a quick list of "You May Be An Empath if…"

- You feel the emotions of others, both good and bad, without even knowing who they are, and sometimes not even being in the same room as them.
- These feelings and energies are not in sync with what is actually going on around you at that moment.
- You tend to your loved ones' needs before your own.
- You sometimes feel like a live wire is going through your body for no apparent reason.
- You sometimes know when someone is sick even before you talk to them.
- You may begin to drown in anxiety and fear when nothing is happening right near you, but you learn of a natural disaster farther away or

even on the other side of the world.

- You sometimes get physical aches and pains for no reason.

Many people are born empaths and do not have the coping skills to deal with these different emotions during childhood. If you are a parent of such a child, please seek help from an expert. As an adult, you can learn meditation techniques to help you cope and filter out some of these complex and often overwhelming energies. Most empaths prefer to live away from people but still have to learn how to protect themselves in a crowd.

Visualization techniques will help as well. A simple one is called the "Light Switch." Picture in your mind's eye a light switch that goes from left to right, something like a dimmer switch. Label one side as "me" and the other as "everyone else." Mentally move the control over to you. You may have to practice this a couple of times a day to help your mind learn to block out or shut out foreign feelings until you are ready to deal with them.

Finally, seeking out a psychic mentor and taking classes can also help you. Speaking to someone who has had the same experiences as you and can help you without judgment is such a relief. Yes, there are reputable places that teach psychics how to control and develop their abilities no matter what they may be.

SIMPLE TECHNIQUES TO HELP YOU DEVELOP YOUR PSYCHIC ABILITIES

Visualization —One of the first things to do is practice your skills. Visualize the emotions you see in those around you and assign them a designation, such as a color. With daily practice, your brain will start to recognize those emotions quickly enough to be able to help others from spiraling down an abyss.

Practice Telepathy—Again, practice the skills you wish to develop. Start slow and small. Choose a friend or relative that you are especially close to. Visualize them in your mind from head to toe, how they walk, talk and even breathe. Send them a short but affirmative message every day, at the same time, for a week. At the end of the week, call them to see if they acknowledge your communication in some way.

Daydream—One of the most powerful instruments we have as humans is our brain. Our minds are capable of so many wondrous and disastrous things. Take time each day to just dream about a future event you would like to happen. See it happening in your mind, every sight, sound, and feeling you might have during that event and picture those involved.

Meditate Daily—Taking time out each day to breathe in and out deeply is a great start to relieving any stressors in your life that may hinder your abilities. Quiet time is essential for our souls to let go of everything for just a little while.

Release Expectations–Not everything you do will work every time. Most things will take a lot of practice, patience, and perseverance. But DO NOT add to your emotional burdens by expecting results every time. If it happens, great; if not, then try again tomorrow. Practice setting goals in your everyday life. Empaths should also practice their psychic abilities. Set a goal of achieving new skills, and practice those skills daily. If you can meet your goals fifty percent of the time, you DO NOT have a fifty percent failure rate; you have a fifty percent success rate.

DO YOU KNOW WHAT CHAKRAS ARE?

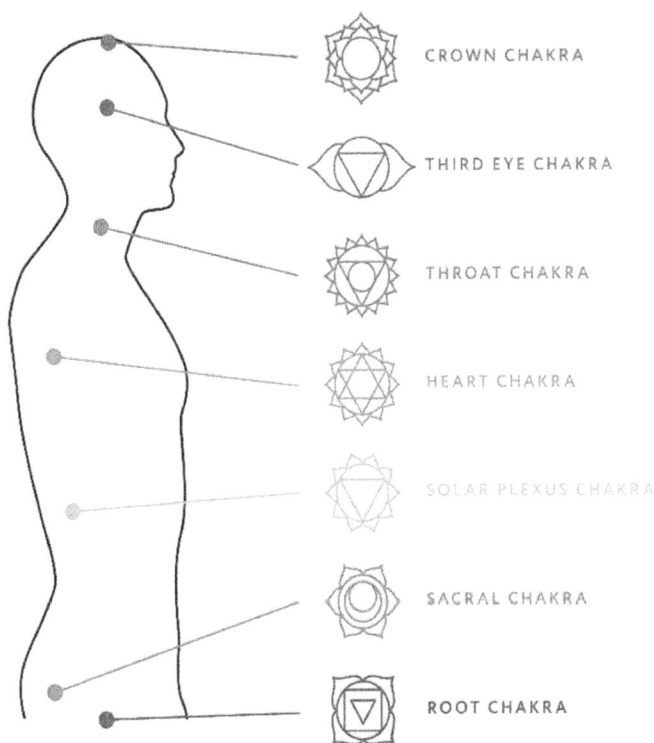

CROWN CHAKRA

THIRD EYE CHAKRA

THROAT CHAKRA

HEART CHAKRA

SOLAR PLEXUS CHAKRA

SACRAL CHAKRA

ROOT CHAKRA

Psychic abilities come from within our bodies, hearts, and minds. What follows is a quick overview of what the Indians have coined the Chakra points in our bodies. These were known as far back as 1500 B.C.- 500 B.C. Some of the exercises we will be discussing involve these particular areas of the body. *Chakra balancing is the process of bringing the spirit, body, and health into harmony.*

Root Chakra −First Chakra−located at the base of the spine, helps us feel grounded.

The Sacral Chakra is located at the base of the Spine. Second Chakra − (Clairsentience) is for emotional expression connected to the lymphatic system.

The Solar Plexus Chakra−Third Chakra−located in the lower abdomen, is where the "gut sensations" come from.

The Chakra of the Heart−Fourth Chakra (Clairempathy)− located at the lower center of the chest, controls emotional healing and mental well-being and is responsible for love, compassion, and forgiveness.

The Throat Chakra − Fifth Chakra (Clairaudience) − located at the base of the neck and controls creativity.

Third Eye Chakra−Sixth Chakra (clairvoyance)−located between the brows and is responsible for information outside the materialistic world.

Crown Chakra − Seventh Chakra (claircognizant) −

located at the top of the head and directs direct communication with all-powerful and conscious energy.

WHAT ARE THE "4 CLAIRS" OF INTUITION?

There are a lot of terms to learn in life for our hobbies, our jobs, and even for everyday living. The psychic realm has its own version of a glossary that we need to absorb to understand others in the field. It is a standard book of knowledge that helps us communicate effectively. These terms have been introduced as they will be used in this book. Once you have mastered them, you will be ready to move to the next part of your learning process. Now, on with the next set of words to know.

- *Clairaudience (hearing voices)* – messages that sound like someone is talking in your mind. Working with other intuitives or reading about intuition actually opens up your own intuition and clairaudient potential.
- *Clairvoyance (seeing images)*–messages arrive as an image or scene in the mind and usually come as a metaphor. So keep looking for images that pop into your mind out of the blue. They may be messages.
- *Clairsentience (recognizing feelings)* – messages come through as a feeling; start journaling these strong feelings and review them over the coming months.
- *Claircognizance (knowing)* – this is when our

brains get an immediate download from our intuition. Start asking your intuition for more information each time a strong feeling overwhelms you.

EXERCISES TO HELP DEVELOP YOUR "CLAIR" SENSES

We have separated the "Clairs" into their respective sections to help keep them uppermost in your mind while doing the following exercises. By following some of our recommended suggestions and at the same time telling yourself that you are now going to practice "Claircognizance", your mind will associate what you are doing with your goal of developing that particular specialty.

Exercising your "hearing voices" or clairaudience

The most straightforward exercise is to meditate daily. Clear your mind, breathe deeply, say a phrase in your mind, remember what you sound like, breathe more deeply, feel each of your chakras – you will hear the sounds around you, let them fade back, and focus on a question inside your mind and ask for guidance, wait, be patient, then hear the message. Make a note of the voice, whether it is male, female, pleasant or unpleasant. Write everything down.

Practice every day for ten to twenty minutes in a quiet place with little or no distractions.

Exercising your "seeing images" or clairvoyance

Linking with your third eye −We have all seen the pictures of someone looking mystical with an extra eye in the middle of their forehead. This is the simplest depiction of your "Third Eye." It is the opening into your mind, your intuitive self, or some may say, just letting your left brain know that you are ready to receive. There is a simple exercise that one of our fellow empaths, Michelle Beltran, has described that help those new to this type of thing.

1. Push your left hand (if you are left-handed, use your right hand) into the middle of your forehead. Then, rotate from left to right (or right to left) a few times. This will help your brain focus on this location.

2. Breath in through your nose and slowly exhale through your mouth.

3. Imagine that pretend eye opening up to see what is happening. To help ingrain this experience into your routine, make a note of the eye's shape and color. For example, are there any eyelashes above or below, and what color are they? Again, it is the little details that help your mind imprint on this moment and what you are trying to accomplish.

4. It may be pretty uncomfortable at first but keep picturing that eye open and ready to receive signals throughout your day.

Visualization bouts - While meditating, pick an item in

your room, and concentrate on it, the shape, the color, the smell, and the feel of it. Then, like daydreaming, your mind will start sending you other images.

Practice using a reading screen – Relax, breathe in and out, close your eyes and visualize a movie screen in front of you. Ask the question of the day, and then let your mind wander. Record what you see.

The truth rose – This is another visualization technique that involves creating a rose in your mind's eye and planting it firmly into the earth. Take note of all the details you created, the color of the rose, the leaves, and the thorns. Then, ask your question and calmly wait. If the rose thrives, then the answer is yes. If it withers, the answer is no.

Exercising your "recognizing feelings" or clairsentience (empaths)

Pay close attention to your emotions – Every day, at least once or twice a day, pay particular attention to how you are feeling in that moment, in that space, and to whatever is going on around you. Recording your impressions will help you cement this practice in your mind.

Watch your physical responses – When something out of the ordinary happens, note where you are physically, who is around you, and how you are feeling. Try this several times in the day, in a different room in your house, at work, or even walking down the street.

Do energy work—Practice healing (sending out healing thoughts to loved ones), meditation (focusing on your own energy), and lightwork (sending positivity out to those around you).

Learn what affects energy —Beginning with the lowest end of the scale, fear, to the highest end, love, you can change the energy in the area you are feeling, by

- Bringing in more natural light
- Clean the area, the objects, people, and animals in the area
- Turn off ALL your electronic devices for a little while to create a space of peace

Practice makes perfect - practice, practice, practice helps you ingrain these "awareness" habits.

Exercising your "knowing" or claircognizance

Automatic writing - Find a cozy place to sit with a pen and a pad, clear your mind, close your eyes, and write for five to ten minutes. Don't look until you feel you are finished.

Sleep with a question under your pillow —Your sleeping mind will work on the question. When you wake up, write down your impressions.

Ask yourself questions with flashcards — Using index cards or card stock, recreate your own deck with the questions on the front and the answers on the back. Prepare five sets of repeated questions with different answers. Concentrate on the question, then let your mind wander.

Meditate to open your Crown Chakra – An important note is that your Root Chakra should be opened first, before the Crown Chakra. The following are some tips to open up your Crown Chakra:

Meditation	Quieting your mind will automatically open up your Crown Chakra - *meditations can be moving meditations, mindfulness sitting meditations or guided meditations.*
Inspiration	What gets you feeling good, hopeful, and, yes, even inspired? Movies, music, the waves in the ocean, a book that makes you smile, or even children or dogs playing? All of these will open up your Crown.
Outdoor Vistas	Find the highest point in nature that you can safely reach, and just sit there and breathe. Looking out over the heights into mother nature's bounty will help open up that Crown too.
Appreciation	Genuine appreciation can be for a well-mowed lawn, fresh air to breathe in deeply, a bold and colorful sunset, or a beautiful painting you can get lost in. These are just a few examples. So what do you truly appreciate?

Head Rubs or Handstands	Whether you just rub your scalp with your hands, have a friend do it, or try standing on your hands, it helps get all that blood flowing in and around your brain.
Acts of Love	Doing small acts out of love can open your Crown Chakra. Nothing gets the heart beating faster, puts a smile on our faces, and helps get the old blood flowing than helping out a stranger. So go ahead and pay for someone's coffee behind you in line or even a meal at the drive-thru. Send a box of donuts to your local firehouse or the police station with a note, "We appreciate all you do." Deliver a pizza to a busy mother in your neighborhood, so she doesn't have to cook that night. These small acts of kindness and love are very effective at opening up the Crown Chakra and more.

Meditate to connect with a claircognizant spirit guide —If you do not already have a guide, you can ask for one by going into a deep meditative state and asking for one. Visualization techniques might also help. Chapter Eight will give you more information on Spirit Guides and how to introduce yourself with exercises to help you learn how to work with them.

CHAPTER SUMMARY

In this chapter, we learned a little bit more about our bodies, their energy centers, and some exercises that we can do to help us develop and improve our psychic abilities. Being a psychic empath should not be overwhelming you or your life. If you take classes to learn more, find a mentor to help you grow, and practice the exercises and techniques we discuss throughout this book, you will not only survive, you will thrive. You will learn to distinguish between your own emotions and those of other people, plants, and even animals.

Being a psychic empath means you really have an extra sense. You can say you have a "sixth sense." It can help you feel the emotional vibrations of all those around you, be they plants, animals, or humans.

In the next chapter, you will learn more about avoiding emotional burnout and energy vampires. There are ways to help you process all these "other" emotions and safe ways to turn them off for a while. You have to take care of yourself first before you can help anyone else. It is crucial to keep this in mind now and in the future.

4

AVOID EMOTIONAL BURNOUT

As an empathic person, there will always be times when you overdo it. You have absorbed too much negative energy and haven't cleansed your psyche in a while. This really should be a daily habit. In some cases, you may even need to help yourself expel all the excess energy two or three times a day. There are quick and simple exercises you can learn and practice until you get to the more in-depth or complicated ones. Some of these you will be able to learn quickly, and some you may not ever want or need to do. If you see an exercise that you do not wish to do now, save it for later. We are all constantly changing and evolving. What works today may not work next week or even next year. So having as many tools at your disposal as possible can only be a good thing.

DEALING WITH THE ENERGIES OF OTHERS

Your best defense is knowledge. When trying to keep yourself from drowning in the emotional malaise of the people around you, acknowledge your skills as an empath. It is important to learn more about these abilities. Learning to trust your own instincts is paramount. And, just knowing your self-worth helps you to set and keep emotional and physical boundaries. Start your day with meditation and repeat it throughout the day if necessary. The key is to "BREATHE" in the good and breathe out the bad as often as needed. Then you will learn ways to transmute all the negative energy into positive energy. Finally, just love yourself for who you are and what gifts you have to share.

WHAT IS AN ENERGY VAMPIRE?

You know about these types of people. They are very similar to the vampires depicted on television and the movies, but instead of blood, they feed on emotional energy. They can quickly drain it out of an empath if you are unwary. The real problem is that anyone can be an energy vampire: a friend, a family member, or perhaps even your spouse. The best way to describe them is by their behaviors. They do not take accountability for anything, they are the drama kings and queens, and they never want to talk about you or your accomplishments, only their own. They can and will use your good nature against you, sucking you into their problems by insinuation, guilt, and even bullying. They are codependent, and you have to break that cycle as quickly as possible.

TYPES OF ENERGY VAMPIRES

The Narcissist–the world revolves around them.

The Rageaholic – only deals with conflict by yelling, accusing, and controlling people.

The Victim – nothing ever works for them, and everyone is against them.

The Drama Queen or King –drama and conflict are like a drug, and they emote often and loudly how they are not at fault.

Control Freaks and Critics – constantly critical of everyone and everything they cannot control or who doesn't do as they say or want.

The Non-Stop Talker–they do not let anyone get in a word during their entire recitation of whatever is going on in their lives.

Passive-Aggressive People–they say they are fine, but you clearly see their real feelings on their faces and through their body language. They smile through their anger.

HOW TO PROTECT YOURSELF FROM ENERGY VAMPIRES

There are several ways you can protect yourself from these different energy vampires, and you can use them simultaneously. You can learn how to turn their behaviors back on them, sometimes through reverse psychology. However, the best methods are the ones that you can control. For instance, set clear boundaries with each one, adjust your expectations, stroke their egos occasionally, limit your exposure, or, finally, just walk away.

SIMPLE TIPS, TRICKS AND TECHNIQUES TO PROTECT YOURSELF AND YOUR PSYCHIC ABILITIES

Using salt in your bath can clear negative energies. You can carry around different crystals on your person or in a bag. Yoga gets you doing the deep breathing exercises, stretching those muscles, and relaxing your entire being while helping you reach a calmer and content state. In general, yoga gets your body moving and relaxes your brain.

Of course, singing lifts your spirits and helps you control your breathing. Try imagining a mirrored ball of light coming into your body to blast away the negative thoughts and feelings, then breathe some more. Using essential oils while relaxing can calm you while doing breathing exercises. Closing your eyes will help shut out distractions while doing more deep breathing. Balance your hormones as you would your chakras on a regular basis. Finally, wean yourself off of caffeine. (Oh, my!)

There are a number of yoga scripts available on the internet that you can use to help you protect yourself and your psychic abilities. There is a reference list at the end of this book which details where these were sourced. We hope you will visit their websites in the future for more of the same.

Cleansing Relaxation Script

What I want for our meditation today is just to release some of that sticky energy, letting go, releasing, and smoothing out the energy field. (Your affirmation)

So, we can have a smoother experience in our lives and a happier one. (Your Goal.)

Start by imagining that you're lying down inside an egg-shaped energy field.

You're in the center of this egg shape: it extends maybe about a foot from your body in every direction.

When you breathe in, you breathe gold light up, around the edge of the egg, and also fill the right side of the egg with gold light.

When you breathe out, you are breathing silver light from the crown of your head all the way down the left side of the egg, filling the left side.

You have the gold light on the right-hand side and the silver light on the left.

Gold relates to solar energy, which is your drive to get things done. Silver energy relates to the lunar, receptive, replenishing energy.

Sit more on your left side; you are on the

giving-back side. You're balancing the two things out with this visualization, too.

You could add a very simple affirmation as the final element. Simply say the affirmation inside yourself in your mind:

I am calm and relaxed.

Use nine breaths and count as you go.

Imagine a smaller egg, about a hand's breadth out from your body. It has two layers, and it represents the energy and emotional bodies.

Keep breathing gold light in and out on the right-hand side, breathing silver light out and down the left-hand side. Keep repeating:

I am calm and relaxed.

Count nine breaths, starting when you're ready...

Now, shrink your attention even further, coming to your spinal cord.

Breathe up and down the length of the spine, coming right up to your brain and then back down.

Breathe nine times, gold light up the length, and silver light down and out. This time say to yourself:

I am at peace

Then, release the focus on the breath and expand your attention to notice how you feel, just a light check on your energy and mental state. (Your Results.)

Cleansing relaxation script - Joanne Sumner Yoga and Meditation Healing

There are other ways you can help yourself a little bit more quickly. Trying different methods will help you not feel stale or in a rut. But, of course, doing the familiar also enables you to center yourself more quickly. We suggest you try a few of the ones below. We then have another meditation script for you to try.

Shielding Visualization

1. Breathe deeply in through your nose and out through your mouth. Repeat a few times.
2. Now, close your eyes and focus on your entire body. Bring down a shimmering cloud of white light that will encase your body. (Most colors will work—use whichever one makes you feel protected.)
3. You may have to repeat this several times: "This shield protects me from everything I do not want to let in."
4. The protection will keep you safe, happy, and feeling good. (Keep breathing in and out as

you say this.)

5. The shields block that which does me harm but will allow in that which is positive.

Calling in the Spirit of the Jaguar—or whichever animal you see as a protector

1. Deep breath in and then out, calming yourself and your energies.

2. Reaching deep inside your heart (helps to picture you doing this)—call out the protective animal spirit. (Choose one like a mountain lion, a bear, a panther, etc.)

3. Picture in your mind's eye her presence, her shape, her coloring, her smell, and her sound as she wraps herself around you.

4. Look into her eyes and know that she will protect you from anyone who tries to intrude upon your internal energy barriers.

Some Things You Can Do to Reduce Your Stress and Create some Positive Energy Around You Throughout the Day

1. Plants, calming nature scenes, and pictures of your pets or loved ones all project positivity for you and your surroundings. Use them liberally at work and home.

2. One of the many plants and herbs that we all could use more of is lavender. It has a lovely scent. The essential oil has calming properties. So use it in your bath, a drop rubbed between your eyebrow, or even burn a handmade

lavender scented candle. All these things can reduce negativity reasonably quickly.

3. At least once a day, go outside and just breathe. Walk in the cool grass, or just walk down a tree-lined trail. Get into nature to break up all those negative vibes sticking to you like an insect.

4. "No." It really is a complete sentence. Get in the practice of using it. Politely, but firmly.

5. A little more self-love throughout your day wouldn't be too out of order either. Treat yourself to a long soak in the tub. Do a dance-off in your living room. Grab the old chocolate fudge and ice cream and make yourself a sundae. (Well, okay, that last one was really all me.)

6. "Time Management." Just saying those two words can send shivers down your spine. It truly is your friend. You have to set boundaries for yourself, your friends, and your family.

Meditation Script: Protecting Your Energy

Meditation Script: Protecting Your Energy I by Meg Sangimino I Soul & Sea I Medium

Release and let go of any and all expectations you have for the day, leaving room for gratitude, compassion, and positivity.

Take a deep breath in. And sigh it all out.

Take a moment to scan your body from head

to toe, evaluating the temperature and cadence of your energy.

Take a few deep breaths, inhale positivity, and exhale negativity.

Long pause.

Bring your awareness to the crown of your head, the crown chakra. Visualize a bright light, full of the energy you have cultivated, shining brightly from this space. A bright, white light surrounds you as you sit or lay in your space. Allow this light to build a protective shield around your body.

Pause.

This is a shield, not to keep others out but to remind you that you control what energy you let in, what boundaries you set, and what external entities you let penetrate your atmosphere.

You are in control of your power.

Visualize this light becoming very close to your body, surrounding your entire self like another layer of skin.

Today, what energy do you want to let in?

What energy makes you feel nourished? Uplifted? Empowered?

Pause.

Today, what energy do you want to fend off?

Shame, guilt, limiting beliefs, and negative thought patterns.

Allow yourself to be in control today. Notice when energy enters your space that makes you feel anything other than love for yourself.

Keep this shield up, not as a defense against anyone, but as a part of you. It is a boundary that shows people how they should appropriately and respectfully interact with you.

It helps you take control of your personal energy; the thought patterns you are prone to; to feel balanced when you think you are spiraling into self-doubt or negative beliefs about yourself.

You are a force.

Every morning, when you wake up, be grateful for the power within you. Protect it with the beautiful gifts you've been given.

As this meditation comes to an end, secure this shield on your physical body, and as you move through your day, let it do its work.

Yoga Can Be Your Friend

The final item in this chapter has to do with yoga. Yes, we have referred to the benefits of various yoga techniques a few times already. Yoga benefits those without any psychic abilities and is really essential for those who do. Yoga is a physical, mental, and spiritual practice created in ancient India. It aims to create a union between the body, the mind, the spirit, and what they call "universal" consciousness. It has been practiced for thousands of years. There must be something to it for it to have lasted this long. It has evolved over the years, but the basic tenets are the same. A couple of exercises that we would recommend from the *Yoga Journal* are de-cording and the Namaste hand exercises.

(de-)Cording

This involves the use of the "Mountain Pose" to begin.

Mountain pose- Tadasana

There are a couple of steps to set up this part and then a few more afterward for the actual de-cording portion. For the Mountain Pose, we are using the instructions from *Yoga Basics.*

- Begin in a standing position, feet together. Lift up, spreading your toes across and then back down.
- You should feel evenly balanced from head to toe.
- Pull up your knees, squeezing your thighs as you go.

- Feel your hips go into alignment directly over your ankles.
- Do not lock your knees.
- Take a deep breath in, lift your waist and push your head towards the ceiling, keeping your spine straight.
- Breathe out and relax your shoulders as you reach towards the floor with your fingers.
- Take a deep breath in as you bring your arms up, and turn your palms, bending at the elbows.
- Breathe out and relax your shoulders again while reaching your fingers up.
- Take a deep breath in and hold for the count of four.
- Breathe out, arms down to your sides.
- And now:
- Close your eyes.
- Let yourself see the energy in your body wrapped in cords all around you.
- Pluck each cord and drop it as you go around your body.
- After the third round, imagine that all your excess energy has been plucked off and any open areas are now closed and filled with your special light.

Namaste Hands

You can do this technique at any time. It helps to center you quickly and can act as a shield as well. You see it done at the end of most yoga exercises too. Simply place your hands in a prayer position (hands flat and palms together in front of the heart): this completes a symbolic circle. Imagine yourself surrounded by your protective light, and your praying hands have closed the circuit to any negative energy that might try to get in as you have released all the bad and brought your favorite colored light back in.

CHAPTER SUMMARY

Throughout this latest chapter, we learned quite a bit about energy vampires, the types of energy vampires, and how to deal with them to protect ourselves. We also explored some different techniques we can use to clean out the overflow of emotions, feelings, traumas, and other energies that have been thrust at us throughout our day. The common thread and the most straightforward advice is to regularly take deep cleansing breaths, protect yourself as much as you can, get out in nature, and set firm boundaries for yourself, your friends, family, clients, and co-workers.

In the next chapter, we will continue on the empath's journey to discover the varied ways to find and keep balance in our lives, now and in the future.

5

FINDING BALANCE AS AN EMPATH

IT'S ALL ABOUT BALANCE

Finding balance in our lives is essential to our emotional as well as physical well-being. Empaths need that to find that delicate balance for themselves even more than other people. They take on the emotions of others, absorbing them into their being; some empaths get lost in others' feelings. Until you can figure out ways to continuously distinguish between your emotions and those you come in contact with or connect with, you will forever feel out of balance. Some of you may even go so far as to retreat from the world altogether. However, there are ways you can begin to help yourself. And you must help yourself before you can help anyone else.

BOLO - BE ON THE LOOKOUT FOR

You and your closest friends might want to become accustomed to looking out for signs that you, as an empath, are becoming overwhelmed by painful emotions so that you can take corrective action as quickly as possible. Some quick signs to look for are:

Chronic fatigue—you are feeling fine, and suddenly you start exhibiting feelings of exhaustion as if you just ran the Boston Marathon or have been swimming in quicksand.

Self-medication – your current feelings of anxiety or depression are becoming so acute and painful that you begin popping pills or drinking more alcohol than usual.

Sudden shift in mood –you are your normal calm self, and suddenly you feel extremely happy, tremendously sad, or very anxious for no apparent reason.

Skin issues –our emotions can be so intense that they begin to affect our outer layer (skin), manifesting in hives, blisters, red spots, etc. when there is no corresponding external influence such as too much sun or chemical exposure.

Panic attacks –yep, these huge emotions hit you like a ton of bricks, and you feel as if you cannot breathe. Again, no apparent physical stimuli.

WHEN TO SET BOUNDARIES

The best time to set boundaries is today. Start today. You can start small and a little at a time, but you have to begin somewhere. For most of our lives, we are taught to be amenable, feel guilty if we ever say "no," and participate in everything asked of us. All empaths struggle with setting boundaries. Some learn early in the game, while others still struggle with the concept every day. These swirling emotions will pierce your protective energy shell and shred it to pieces if you do not set some basic boundaries in your life with your friends and coworkers. It will take time, practice, patience, and strength of will to learn your particular limits, how to set them in a loving and caring manner, and then "STICK TO THEM," even when you feel guilty and want to relent.

HOW TO SET BOUNDARIES

How you set your boundaries will take some time, experimentation, and research on your part. With pen and paper in hand (probably a couple of composition books and your favorite blue or black ink pens), begin investigating what you would like those boundaries to be. Only you can understand your own situation, your current lifestyle, your workload, your family dynamics, and your ability to self-care daily to begin setting your own boundaries. Once you determine what they should be, you have to WRITE THEM DOWN and keep them in a prominent place where you will see them every day.

You may add to them, decrease them, or revise them in the future. That is perfectly fine. They are your boundaries, after all. The next step will be to implement those boundaries in your everyday life.

Don't agree to anything in the moment—Get into the habit of not answering requests right away. Explain that you will have to check your calendar and will get back to their request the next day. No, this may not work in all situations, but if those around you know that you always want a 24-hour thinking time for every request, they will eventually fall in line or fall away. You are showing respect for their needs at that moment. You will just have to figure out if what they are asking of you will make you happy and if you really have the time and inclination to do what they are asking of you and if it will help you and them.

Find a few kind, compassionate ways to say no – Saying "no" is difficult. We are hardwired to say "yes" to our parents, grandparents, and bosses. But when we get older and have to learn to fend for ourselves, we learn to say "no" when what is being asked is not something we truly wish to do. You should write down and practice several loving, kind, compassionate, and respectful ways of saying "no."

Here are a couple of tips to help you

Firstly, you need a calendar, paper, or electronic, whichever one you will actually use. Mark out times for yourself first. Yes, you have to schedule those activities that help you take care of yourself before anyone else, such as your meditation period, exercise time, and "mental health" activities. Whatever they may be for you. Then mark out all of your working hours and any family commitments. Once that is done, you will have a better picture of what times and days you have available. You will be surprised just how little time you actually have.

There are a couple of ways of saying "no" using your calendar. First, you can say that you are already committed on that day and time. It does not matter if that is your "me" time or not; it is already spoken for. You are working at that time; you have a family commitment you just cannot miss; you have a doctor's appointment then; (we all know how hard it can be to get an appointment); the kids are out of school that week, so your time is committed to them. Be honest about your time commitments when you say "no" to someone. Especially if you do not want to do whatever they ask of you. It helps if you practice a couple of different ways of saying it to be prepared based on what is being asked of you. However, sometimes you just have to say "no thank you" and move on.

Secondly, once you have a list of handy "no" scripts, you will probably need to practice the following:

- "It is okay to say 'no' to what I do not wish to do."
- "I have already committed myself for that date and time."
- "I have to take care of myself first. No one is being helped if I have neglected myself."

Saying those things yourself, printing it out on a piece of paper, hanging it next to your computer, and wherever you answer your phone is important. In addition, it might be a good idea to have little reminders on your phone that pop up at odd hours of the day. These are simple to create using the calendar function on your phone. You can even allocate sounds to each reminder. Yes, just like assigning a specific ringtone for your partner, children, or even your parental units. It will help to reinforce the fact that you are important too.

Third and final suggestions are that you can always revisit their request later. If there is something you would really like to help with but are not sure when you will have the time, tell them just that. If it is something they can reschedule to another day, then ask them to suggest other dates and times that might work. You can always say that you might know of someone that can take your place at that activity or event, and you will make inquiries for them. (Only if you do know of someone who can help them with whatever is being asked.) Again, this is only when you want to assist but cannot due to previous commitments.

Preparing yourself to say "no" is good for your mental well-being and keeping the lines of communication open with those you care about. Being able to say "no" gracefully prevents you from over-committing yourself and will also help those who ask feel appreciated and understood. You are as important as anyone else on this planet and deserve to be able to enjoy your time in this world yourself to become a better version of "you" along the way.

EXERCISES TO HELP YOU GET YOUR LIFE INTO BALANCE AND SET YOUR BOUNDARIES

Now let's get down to the fun stuff. There are many different ways to get your life into balance and establish and maintain boundaries. After all, if you set boundaries, you will, in turn, find your balance. For example, the first set of exercises might be:

Develop your boundaries – Write these things down. Your mind will begin to work on them subconsciously if you have them posted where you can see them daily.

Be aware of your body–Your body is a machine, a finely tuned instrument. You have to learn how to keep it healthy, both physically and emotionally. It should become a daily habit. (Can you say SELF-CARE?)

Balance your nervous system–Absorbing other people's emotional energy all day can throw your nervous system out of whack. You can get that machine back in working order through daily meditation, long walks in nature, and other daily self-care rituals.

Learn to regulate intimacy – Whether you are hiding from intimacy or are deeply involved in relationships, you will need to practice allowing people in or how to keep them out. There is a happy medium for you and your empathic self. You just have to try not to overdose or starve yourself in the meantime.

Develop emotional immunity – Just like learning to say "no," sometimes you have to develop a shield to keep away other people's emotions. This, too, takes time, practice, and patience, but with breathing exercises, yoga, and other self-care methods, you can teach yourself how to shield yourself when necessary.

Become aware of how you handle situations – In this exercise, you will begin to visualize different situations where you might have needed to set some boundaries. Try to remember the entire event. Write down what you remember. Then start working on ways that you could have changed the outcome by setting some boundaries in a kind and loving way. You will probably have to do this type of analysis every day for a while to get in the habit of recognizing the different ways YOU can make subtle changes in the way you handle different situations. Practice is the best learning tool.

Boundaries for empaths and owning your body are a right – We all have a perceived "personal boundary space" around our bodies. We do not like it when someone invades this space uninvited. It is the same for empaths. Other people's emotions can slip into our energy fields and disrupt our sense of harmony. You have the RIGHT to control that aspect of your being. Unless you are incarcerated, you have the right to decide what happens in and around your body. This is where learning some deep breathing, self-care, and self-talk techniques come into play. Breathing deeply in and then out and saying, "I'm in control of what happens to my body" as a kind of mantra should help raise your shields and keep unwanted emotional turmoil at bay. It is up to you to decide if you want to quickly access the other person's emotional state and just as quickly move back to consider if you can help them.

Empath boundaries: Learn to trust yourself – Since empaths are, by nature, highly perceptive and intuitive, they are naturally the quieter ones in the group. Experience has taught them to doubt their intuition and perceptions even though they are usually right. Learning to trust yourself, your instincts, and your intuition is paramount for an empath's equilibrium. This cannot be stressed enough. You have to learn to trust yourself and your abilities. Yes, these may be just emerging, and you are still learning. But, as with all things in this life, you are human, you make mistakes, and you have to take a chance on yourself!

Take care of yourself first – before attempting to help anyone else. This really should be self-explanatory, but as deeply caring individuals, we tend to jump in to help other people before making sure we are safe and in a position to help them. If you have ever flown on an airplane, you would have heard the safety speech about always putting on your own oxygen mask first before putting one on your child, family member, or seatmate. This applies to ALL empaths as well.

Putting empath boundaries into practice –You have done all the research and established some boundaries you need for yourself, and now the only thing left to do is…PRACTICE.

SELF-CARE IS TOO IMPORTANT TO IGNORE

Here is a list of some of the things you might want to do for yourself to help you maintain your balance every day of your life:

Put yourself first– As with everything in life, you have to take care of yourself first.

Set Boundaries–If you do not consistently apply your boundaries, you will lose your sense of balance.

Let it go–One of the hardest things most of us have to do is just let go of things that no longer work, people that are not good for us, and situations we cannot control.

Process your own emotions–If you cannot differentiate your own emotions and feelings from those of others, you are in trouble. You have to learn to separate your feelings from those around you to help those you want to help.

Practice celebrating –Find something to celebrate every single day. It does not have to be big, and it does not have to be about you. Just get in the habit of celebrating your victories and achievements and those of others.

Stop absorbing other emotions — Yes, we know that is what you do. You are, after all, an empath. But you have to cleanse your aura and expel all that other energy from your field on a regular basis. It builds up like sludge in your sinks and can completely clog your emotional energy field. When you need to keep others out, visualize a wall that blocks them out. Ask for protection (from whichever divine being you believe in), wear appropriate crystals on your person, say positive affirmations, and wear something blue if you need a quick fix. The color blue affects your emotional being.

Implement self-care into your daily routine — There are several ways to help you with this through regular meditations and affirming what you are truly grateful for that day. Journaling is a great way to release all emotions. Some empaths even practice various nature rituals. Learn about them and practice them. Then, see what works for you.

Mental and physical health need equal attention — Keeping yourself mentally and psychically fit should become a daily routine. Your body needs this to keep healthy. You know this. Do this in any way that works for you. Some believe in traditional Chinese medicine and a herbal regime. Others prefer following the recommendations of a health nutritionist. Do whatever fits into your lifestyle. There is nothing like regular exercise for your body.

CHAPTER SUMMARY

It is essential to create and maintain a healthy balance in your emotional and physical being; it will also affect your psychic well-being. Learn what your emotional boundaries need to be in order to become a healthy, practicing empath. Discover those boundaries through your own research and experimentation, and practice them daily. There are different exercises to help you figure out how to create those boundaries, apply them, and use them regularly. Only by determining what works for you and your life and putting those things to work for you will you maintain your balance as a healthy human being and caring, giving empath.

In the next chapter, you will learn more about empaths, their inability to really see their true worth, and why their abilities should be regarded as a gift. Many empaths feel misunderstood, and their pain goes unnoticed by everyone around them. We hope to educate them about these emotions, help them see their true worth, and give them simple exercises they can incorporate into their daily lives to build up their self-esteem.

LET'S TAKE A BREAK FOR SOMETHING IMPORTANT!

It's easy to think that our individual actions don't matter in the big picture, but nothing could be further from the truth. Every action we take has an impact, however small, on the world around us.

In this case, a simple review can help an empath break free from the feeling of being overwhelmed and live a life of meaning and purpose.

You don't need to spend any money to help, but your review will be invaluable to me as an author in my mission of helping as many empaths as possible.

Just sixty seconds of your time is all it takes to make a massive difference in someone else's life. You can help empower someone to make better decisions and live an empowered life with just a few words.

Your review will also be a beacon of hope for others who are feeling overwhelmed and unsure of where to turn. It will show them that they're not alone in their struggles and that they can find the guidance they need to break free and live a meaningful life.

So please, leave a review of the book and its content.

Your review will help make a difference in the lives of countless empaths, and you'll never know the full impact of your action. But it will be a big one, I assure you!

By leaving your review, you'll help to change the world, even if this means helping one empath at a time.

Click on this and you will be taken to the book page, then scroll down and click on the "Write a customer review" option.

Review this product

Share your thoughts with other customers

Write a customer review

Thank you!

6

HOW TO BUILD SELF-ESTEEM AS AN EMPATH

A Typical Empath's Story

An empath named Emily had a hypersensitive personality. She was a people-pleaser in that she loved to be needed by others and help them in any way she could. It brought her joy. And it also brought her validation, as if that was her sole purpose in life.

In her youth, she had a succession of relationships that didn't seem to last long. One even turned violent at one point. And always, it was the other party that left her with parting words like, "You just don't seem to be fully committed in this relationship." Or "You spend more time with your friends than me, so I'm moving on." As time progressed, the parting comments became worse, as did the type of men she chose to date.

In friendships, she was the type of person who, as we said, loved to be needed. So she found herself playing counselor to many people. And she would call these people friends. But strangely, they only came to her, wanting to spend time with her, when they needed advice, a willing ear, or a shoulder to cry on. And afterward, they would leave with empty promises of getting together again soon.

Somehow, even with all the people around her, a piece of her always felt alone and empty. This is because there was no one there to see her cry, no one to console her, and no one to see beyond the mask she wore for the world.

Added to this was the constant weight she carried from all of those she had helped and interacted with; the problems and the emotions (sorrow, anger, fear, pain). They mingled with her feelings, often casting her into internal confusion and chaos.

And slowly, it began to erode or chip away the fragile self-esteem she had built for herself based on the help she gave to others. Until, one day, she found herself in a state of depression where she felt worthless. And she

> felt her life stagnating. (Taken from "Empathic Perspectives")

As you read through this tale, you might be saying, "I feel that way too." Even though you may have not been personally abused in all the ways listed above, you will have questioned your self-worth at one time or another. You may have sasked, "What am I really worth to my friends, family, and lovers?" You might have asked a more profound philosophical question "Why am I here?" That is another deep, dark question many people ask themselves. Now that you have made it this far, you must commit to improving your mental and physical well-being to answer these and other questions. Make a conscious effort to seek guidance from professionals, mentors, and trusted friends.

WHAT IS SELF-ESTEEM?

Self-Esteem is simply how we think of ourselves. For most of us, our self-esteem is centered on how our family and friends see us. For others, their self-esteem is centered on material possessions. For the empath, their self-esteem is all about how they can help others. They see themselves as failures or successes depending on how many people they have helped, how much emotional turmoil they have diffused, and how many friends and family members have come to them for help.

They take on the emotional baggage of those around

them long before they learn how to protect themselves, know their own emotions from those of others, and how they truly see themselves. Separating all these takes time, attention to yourself, practice, and even professional help. There is nothing wrong with seeking help from professionals. They can help guide you through discovering your own emotions, cleaning out everyone else's, and building up your self-image. After all, if you cannot help yourself first, how will you ever help others? Put it another way. If you do not know your own worth, how will anyone else discover and appreciate it?

EMPATHS ARE MORE PRONE TO DEPRESSION AND ANXIETY

If you do not have a good handle on your self-worth, especially as an empath, you too will be prone to bouts of depression or anxiety. Both these conditions, when left untreated, can develop into debilitating "rumination" cycles, which we will talk about next.

"The depressed person dwells on losses and missteps from the past, while the anxious ones drown in a sea of 'what if' questions."

The first thing most of us need to do is recognize the signs and symptoms of depression and anxiety. Your abilities to absorb both the negative and positive emotional energies of those around you will worsen these conditions. They build on top of your own. Once you have educated yourself on identifying these warning signs, you will develop ways to help you come out of them as quickly as possible. The main tools in the empath's arsenal are breathing exercises and visualization. Take some time to identify if these feelings are yours or someone else's. If they do not belong to you, then lovingly send them back to where they came from. If they are yours, talk to your therapist to help you with your current situation.

STOP RUMINATIONS IN THEIR TRACKS

One thing that both depression and anxiety have in common and which affects our self-esteem is ruminating thoughts. Negative things tend to run on and on in our heads. Our "self-talk" sometimes has us chewing on a problem or situation like a cow chewing on a cud—over and over and over again until we run screaming down the long hallway of our minds. This is definitely not a good thing for anyone but especially for an empath. You suffer from low self-esteem, you worry that you are not helping people enough, you are not good enough at your skills, people do not like you for who you are, and on and on until you are no longer in control of yourself or your emotions. Coming back from this type of problem is not a short, quick fix. Basically, you have been training your brain to keep reinforcing these unproductive thoughts, ideas, and feelings. As a result, your body suffers, as do your physical and psychic energies.

Once you recognize that you are ruminating over a

situation, you can learn to remove yourself from this destructive cycle and turn it into something positive or constructive. In other words, try to stop it before it gets too far and then turn the negative thinking into a problem that can be solved. Rephrase it. Distract yourself by doing something creative; start cleaning, go outside, and breathe. Another technique would be to write it all down in your journal. Journaling all your thoughts and feelings lets them escape from your head and onto the paper. It is surprising how effective that can be. Next, you can do something you wouldn't normally do, like turning on the stereo, dancing or singing a couple of songs. Finally, seek professional help if you cannot cut off the repetitive negative thoughts.

Ruminating is bad for you. Nip it in the bud fast. You are a good person. You are worth the love and attention you give yourself and receive from others. Identify your problems and work on them one at a time. Congratulate yourself for every success, whether small or great. They are all worthy of praise. Do things that YOU enjoy doing as often as possible. Create a network of friends and family that support YOU and not just your abilities.

SELF-LOVE IS IMPORTANT FOR EMPATHS TOO

Is loving yourself first really too radical to consider? No, not really. You have to be able to love yourself before you can love someone else. That is a commonsense saying that my grandmother has been telling me since I was a youngster. A healthy amount of self-love may be hard to define. It takes time, effort, and practice to define your own parameters and learn to implement changes in your life that help you as a person. As an empath, learn to love who and what you are. You are worth knowing and loving.

Empaths do require a slightly different kind of self-love than most people. Their ability to absorb positive and negative feelings will drain their emotional well of energy. They will need more "alone time," "me time," and sometimes just more sleep than your average person. They need to recharge, reflect, and dispel all excess emotions on a daily basis. They, too, struggle with low self-esteem, seek validation of their worth from others, are their own worst critic at times, and have difficulty accepting compliments of any kind. They talk negatively about themselves rather than building themselves up with self-talk.

Try some of these things to help you get started with strong self-love practices:

Deal with your past traumas – Most empaths have significant traumas in their lives. Traumas tend to increase awareness of our psychic abilities. To help you become a healthier and more productive empath, acknowledge these traumas, deal with them, and decide they are no longer a part of your life. This will go a long way to help you develop healthy self-love habits. Traumas will have less and less impact on your emotional energy. You will become a healthier you.

Understand why you're here – Now, that is an age-old question. Why are we here? What are we meant to do with our lives? Understanding what you want out of life is a major step in discovering your self-love quotient, i.e., how much you love yourself. If you know what you want, where you want to go, and how you will journey to get there, then you have a plan, and that is better than floundering around like most humans do throughout their lives.

Practice self-affirmation – This is another type of "train your brain" exercise. When you practice positive affirmations, you help manifest those things in your life. You set the tone for your human journey by what you practice and believe. You train your brain by declaring that you are a good person, a healthy person, a seeker, or even just a believer. Visualize those qualities and words in your head every day. Look at pictures of nature, write down positive sayings and quotes, and display them everywhere so that you see them all the time. There is a saying in the computer world, "GIGO, or garbage in, garbage out," so vice versa is true as well. Self-affirmations direct your focus toward your strengths

Set healthy boundaries and protect your energy – We discussed establishing healthy boundaries to protect your energy in a previous chapter. I like the visualization technique where you see a protective field all around your body, and your raised hands are the only entrance you allow for others' energy to enter. It's like keying on the computer. Your hands do all the typing, and you just interpret what you see.

REMEMBER to return to the sender what energy you received and take back whatever energy you sent out.

Learn to reduce anxiety—Feeling anxious is just part of life. It helps us know when we need to pay attention to what is happening around us. Our instincts kick in and say, "HEY! Pay Attention." However, when those feelings turn to fear and unease, this is anxiety. These feelings can get out of control if we let them. For example, the sense that we are paralyzed into inaction, will never be good enough, cannot speak, and melt into a pool of dread. The simplest way to deal with this is with breathing exercises and visualizations that better things can and will happen.

Rest and recharge without guilt—yes, you are an emotional go-getter—a bad-ass empath who has developed a healthy habit of self-love. Do not forget to rest. This simple habit can help you to improve your life. You DO NOT have to feel guilty for taking the time you need to relax and recharge. The world will still be there when you are ready and will benefit more from your help when you feel rested and refreshed.

TIPS AND EXERCISES TO HELP YOU BUILD SELF-ESTEEM – A LITTLE BIT EVERY DAY

You are human; you have a past you are dealing with,

a present that needs your attention, and a future waiting for you to claim it. You are the one who has control over your self-esteem. No one can or has the right to determine your worth. You decide that for yourself. You have to learn, grow, practice what you have learned, love yourself, and show self-compassion at all times. The road to self-discovery takes a lifetime and doing a little bit every day will help you achieve your goals. Only then can you begin to really help others.

Know the goal – Set your own goals. Writing them down is a good start. Work on them every day.

Accept your tricky brain – your brain is your best friend and your worst enemy. You have to train it with good habits to break all the bad ones you have learned over the years.

Tune into your thoughts – you will be surprised at all the negative thoughts inside your head. Write them down on sticky pads and order them from the loudest to the softest (both good and bad). Rearrange them with the ones you want to be loudest in front and put the softest ones towards the back. Get rid of the ones you don't want.

Support your mind with your body – a healthy body helps your mind be healthy. So get plenty of exercise, fresh air, eat healthily, etc.

Step outside yourself – when you have been in your

head too much, step out for a while and do something crafty, some yoga, or just take a walk in the woods.

Treat yourself as you would a friend—we should all treat ourselves and do something just for fun with a friend. Do something silly or creative, dance, sing, or just enjoy the day.

Watch your tone —remember that talking to yourself in a sarcastic or hurtful tone is just as bad as talking to someone else in that tone. You would not do that to a friend or even a stranger without provocation. So why do it to yourself?

Turn up another voice – Negative self-talk can be countered by visualizing talking to another person you consider a guide, mentor, or friend who can turn those negatives into positives or at least a constructive problem you can solve. Practice this every time negative thoughts start percolating, and your brain will form a new, more positive habit.

Foster the Flow of Compassion – you naturally treat others with compassion. Heck, you treat most animals with kindness and respect. You need to develop those habits with yourself as well. Yes, you may have done something wrong but you are human and you deserve as much or more compassion than you give to a complete stranger.

Acknowledge the forces against you —there is good and evil in the world. You can only deal with what is in front of you. You cannot change the world. You can only make yourself a better human being, a more effective empath, and, hopefully, help those in your sphere of influence. Some things are just out of your control. Try to know the difference.

Embrace the power of practice – You have to practice all the techniques discussed so far as they pertain to you and your situation. Of course, not everything will work, and not everything is right for you. But with practice and patience, in time, you will develop your skills and be able to handle your own emotional energies and learn how to help others effectively.

FORGIVENESS

The expression *"To err is human; to forgive, divine"* is a *famous line by English poet Alexander Pope from his poem, An Essay on Criticism, Part II, written in 1711.* We need to apply that phrase to ourselves. Yes, we may have forgiven everyone in our lives who has ever wronged us in some way. But, for some reason, we forget to do that for ourselves. It may sound problematic, I know, but it is still true. We seem to dwell on our own mistakes far more than on others. Well, maybe except for our siblings. I am still mad at my brother for telling a fib about me that got me in trouble when we were five or six, and he passed away quite a few years ago. Anyway, you have to begin routing out all these swirling guilty feelings about what you have done or said and move on.

Journal About Your Emotions and Don't Hold Back

Here is a suggestion that might appeal. Get a dark-colored composition book. Record everything you have been hiding about things you have done wrong, people you have mistreated, and bad things you have said that still bother you. Write down all the details you can remember, the feelings, sights, and even the sounds. Now say to yourself, "I have learned from these experiences and will not repeat them in the future." Then take the book outside and burn it. Watch all those things just go up in smoke and blow away. The ceremonial burning routine is wonderful.

Recognize Thoughts of Self Condemnation and Replace Them

If you feel there are recurring or even new offenses, try rephrasing them into a positive. Yes, I did this thing, but now I know what not to do or say about that in the future.

Roleplay: Pretend the Offender Was Someone Else

These days, many of us find ourselves in front of a mirror talking to ourselves. Self-talks, pep-talks, talking ourselves out of dating that sketchy person, or whatever. Some even record the sessions to put them on a social media page. But for our purposes here, why not pretend the person in the mirror is someone else? You can more easily forgive someone else. Use positive words and reinforce the emotions of well-being that are now directed at yourself. Your brain sees your face and thinks, "Oh, I guess I need to forgive, forget." And then and move on.

Write Yourself a Letter of Forgiveness

It cannot be stressed enough that the simple act of writing things down can help you deal with things so you can move on. If you need to remember something –write it down. Your brain reinforces the things you have written by hand through your eyes as you repeat them to yourself. If you need to get rid of recurring thoughts inside your head–write them all down. Write a letter to yourself describing what you did that was wrong and why you think you did it, but reiterating that you have learned from that experience and are now moving on to something better and new.

Write Down How Your Mistake Has (Or Can) Make You a Better Person if You Let It

Again (so very popular), write down everything about the mistake, the deed, or the conversation that went wrong, who was there, where you were, the sights and sounds, and then rephrase the entire scenario into a learning situation. For example, I did this thing, but I learned not to do it again. Or how I turned this conversation or deed into something positive that has helped me know more about myself.

Quote Self-Forgiveness Affirmations Daily

Affirmations are short, simple, positive sentences that

help our brains to grab onto concepts quickly. Start saying them over and over. It helps train our thought processes to do things better and become a better version of ourselves. Writing or typing these affirmations, then posting them on our walls, sitting in a stack on our coffee table, or adding to our daily reminders before meditation, exercising, and even before we fall asleep, ingrains them into our being.

Self-forgiveness is a choice. I choose to forgive myself.	*I am forgiven.*
I acknowledge my faults and completely forgive myself.	*I am loved.*
I am done beating myself up. What happened is in the past.	*I am a good person.*

Try not to let your mistakes define who you are. You are human, just like every other person on this little blue ball. You deserve to be forgiven for your faults, but you must also learn from them and grow and change. Cleaning out this closet of destructive and negative thoughts will help you become a better empath and a better human being.

CHAPTER SUMMARY

Like everyone else on this planet, empaths experience low self-esteem. Their abilities may make them more prone to depression and anxiety, exacerbated by not having a healthy self-worth quotient. Most empaths develop their skills following some significant traumas in their lives. Their instinct and inherited abilities will show themselves earlier in life because of this. They are not taught healthy ways to deal with other people's emotions, let alone their own.

Learning about the many pitfalls in your emotional journey as an empath, techniques to recognize the signs and symptoms of negative emotions, and exercises and habits to convert them into healthy ones is all good. In addition, appreciating your self-worth and learning how to effectively employ self-love techniques will assist you in your voyage in life.

In the next chapter, you will learn more about intuition and how you can develop your skills to help others.

7

INTUITION – HOW TO TAP YOUR INNER WISDOM

According to Merriam Webster Online Dictionary – **Intuition is** *the power or faculty of attaining direct knowledge or cognition without evident rational thought and inference. Whereas insight is the capacity to gain an accurate and deep intuitive understanding of something.* Thus, intuition comes before insight for most humans.

THE SCIENTIFIC POINT OF VIEW

Scientists have been trying to prove and measure intuition for years. Psychologists and neuroscientists are still trying to understand it, even today. Recently, through extensive testing, MRIs, and lots of data analysis, various scientists around the world have determined that there are actually three "brains" in the human body that collect and process every kind of stimuli around us.

The head, heart, and gut all have their own set of neurons that process what is happening around us every day. They read the people around us, their emotional clues, body language, the words they have chosen to use, and how they say them. All these combine to kick off our intuitive selves so we can reach logical insights and problem solve. This is more than the old "fight or flight" type of information. Although intuitions are not one hundred percent accurate all the time as they are based on the information presented to us at that moment, they do serve a greater purpose. Rick Snyder sums up the scientific study best in his article. "Head, Heart, and Gut: The Three Brains that Control Intuition."

The card below best summarizes most of the findings

Cephalic Brain (Head)

- 86 billion neurons
- The seat of language, cognition, consciousness, and creativity
- Recognizes, gives meaning, and creates narratives.
- "I think," "I reckon," "I understand."

Cardiac Brain (Heart)

- 40,000 neurons that can operate independently from the head brain
- Handles emotional processing, expression of values, and interpersonal connections
- "I feel," "My heart says," "Heavy/light heart."

Enteric Brain

- 100 million neurons
- Controls self-preservation and mobilization, responds to challenges, opposition and danger
- Determines core sense of self
- "It takes guts," "my gut tells me."

The scientific aspect relates particularly to women. This has been proved by three different scientific studies conducted in different areas of the world and in different years. Women have a greater capacity for intuitive processing. Women's corpus callosum, the connective white matter that connects our left and right brain hemispheres, is thicker than men's. This allows them to form more intuitive insights and, with practice, these "feelings" can become more accurate. Women have historically been more able to express their emotions, whereas men have always been taught to suppress them. This physical attribute connects the left and right brains and allows gut feelings and intuition to connect to the logical informational gathering areas. Basically, women's brains have superpowers and are optimized for rapid, intuitive decision-making.

The prevailing consensus, especially in these days of rapid sensory overload and the informational dumps we get from social media and "supposed" accurate news outlets online, is that we need to develop our intuition more than ever. We may not be running from physical predators as much as we used to, but there are dangers our inner selves are trying to protect us from. So, pay attention to those queasy or butterfly feelings you get from your gut or those shaking heart sensations when deciding what the correct thing to do is. Ask those questions to your inner selves, "Is this the right thing to do?" Wait for a beat and see if your unconscious mind sends signals through your neurons to proceed or bail out. They may just be trying to save you.

THE SPIRITUAL POINT OF VIEW

From a spiritualist or spiritual point of view, intuition is that small voice inside you trying to help you along your life's journey. It embodies all your past life experiences, what you have been through in this life, and what you hope to achieve going into the next one. It is not the logical part of yourself and is more than your instinctual being. Instead, it comprises information and sensation gathered through your head and processed through your heart and gut.

A true intuitive leap feels light and productive or non-harmful. However, it may trigger your logic senses that tell you not to do something. Those are your fears and insecurities trying to horn in on the decision. There are ways to know when your intuition is trying to get your attention, and there are exercises to do that can help you develop trust in what your feelings are trying to convey. Intuition is like any other muscle in your body or psychic skill you wish to enhance. You have to practice, practice, practice. And with patience, persistence, and experimentation, you, too, can develop your intuitional superpowers.

HOW TO KNOW WHEN TO TRUST YOUR INTUITION?

There are several ways to recognize the signs of intuition. Depending on what is happening in your life at the moment and the decisions you are facing, you may get feelings of dread (don't do this or that); you feel lighter and inspired (do this or that); you keep seeing patterns in your everyday routines (Hey! Pay attention to this); or you may even start having vivid dreams. Yep, that is your unconscious working on problems while you sleep. Your heart and brain want you to achieve your goals in life; they are just both trying to work out a way for you to achieve them. Not all logic is bad. It forms part of how your thought processes work to fulfill your expectations. Whereas intuition helps you figure out where to start.

If you genuinely wish to develop your intuitive skills and begin to trust them more in your daily decision-making, you will need to start recording your reactions, the feelings, the images, and anything else that occurs when you hear the still, small inner voice. Your intuition needs silence to become more effective. So, meditations, deep breathing, and clearing your mind of distractions is always a good way to start. Keep your pen and journal or notebook handy at all times to record what you see in your mind's eye and feel in that moment. If you dream about something, write down what you saw and how you felt when you wake up. Make a note if you notice a pattern of information, objects, or even people you keep seeing.

Processing this information, making decisions, and recording your results may seem like what cold-hard scientists do. But, any person seeking knowledge should use the tools that work to achieve the goals they wish to achieve. As empaths, we want to develop trust in our intuition and intuitive muscles to move forward in this life and help as many people as we can. Most of us just want to have as many "good" tools as possible in our arsenal to live happy and productive lives. Your inner light wants to help you achieve those goals.

EXERCISES TO DEVELOP INTUITION

There are several different exercises you can do on a regular basis to help develop your intuition and feel more confident in trusting it. Some may work for you, and some may not. Do not be discouraged; just keep trying different things, and soon enough, you will develop some mighty fine intuitive muscles.

1. *Practice asking for guidance*—You can ask direct questions of your intuition. You may not get an answer right away. Start by taking calming, deep breaths in and then out. Think quickly about what you want to ask, and then just let it go. You may or may not get a feeling right away. The point is to make a habit of soliciting answers and believing that they will come

when it is time.

2. *Observe* – Journaling, making notes and observations are all part of learning new and exciting skills. Practice observing what you see during a meditation session, listen with your heart, and record some of your impressions. Check back later and compare what you wrote down with what you have experienced throughout your day.

3. *Ask* – bedtime practice – This is a great way to let your unconscious mind help you out while resting. Calm your mind, breathe deeply in and then out. Ask your question clearly and say to yourself, "I know I will have an answer by morning." Write down your question and then just relax and fall asleep. A positive confirmation that you know your brain and heart will come up with something is great practice. Yes, sometimes it may not work, but if you continue to try and believe that it will, it will eventually start working on a more regular basis.

4. *Learn to quiet your mind* – One of the hardest things we all have to do is let everything go and just let ourselves rest. Clearing your brain and breathing in and out for a few seconds each day will help declutter all your emotions and running thoughts. Practice at least once or two a day with no goal or question in mind.

5. *Practice a sense of gratitude* – It is amazing how much positive feedback you can receive from

your own self by being grateful for what you have, who you have in your life, what you are doing and able to accomplish, and the simple act of being here, wherever you might be at that moment in time. Be grateful that the air is clean, the water is cool or warm depending on your needs, the food you have to eat, the friends you see every day, the clothes that keep you warm and protected from the elements, and the abilities that you are developing each and every day. Writing down three things that you are grateful for or about each day brings you more of the same and even better things to come.

6. *Creative visualization*–This skill is an important tool for your skillset. It becomes the "go-to" method for achieving what you want in the future. Utilizing your imagination can help you see where you want to go, who you want to be with, and who you want to help. Using your mind's eye to create strong mental images helps your unconscious self work on them to help achieve your goals. It does take practice, and you should never feel self-conscious about wanting to be healthy, having enough money to pay your bills, travel when and where you want, and even be able to create beautiful things to share with others. These are all part of your journey through this life.

7. *Free writing* – Now, this is a fun way to experiment, with no consequences. You just

grab a couple of pieces of paper and some writing instruments. Sit at a comfortable table and clear your mind of everything. Then just begin to write. No judgments, no editing, no filter. Just let everything flow for as long as you would like. When you feel you are done, take a moment, breathe deeply in and out to clear off any tension you have built up, and read what you have. It may not make sense, but it helps to clear out your brain. Check back in a few days to see if anything you have written pertains to anything you have experienced over the last couple of days. This is like automatic writing.

8. *Wake without an alarm* – This is another fun exercise to help train your unconscious mind and intuition to help you wake up on time. Practice for a couple of days. Tell yourself before going to bed that you will wake up at a specific time and BELIEVE it to be so. After a couple of tries, when it starts to work, you will be saying to yourself, "Hey, my intuition is working and can be trusted."

9. *Guess who's calling?* – Another fun thing to do several times a day is guess who is calling, texting, or messaging you. It is cheating, though, if you have a unique ring or text tone for that person. You just want to allow your intuitive self to have the chance to sense who is trying to contact you at that moment. Keep trying and practicing as often as you can. It is

just another way to flex those intuition muscles.

10. *Play memory games* – Whether you make your own cards, use regular playing cards, or even purchase the game Memory from your local store, playing this by yourself or with some friends is a fun way to build up those memory muscles and intuition.

11. *Play the Stratego game*–I used to love this game as a kid. It is another guessing game but can be used to develop your intuition and memory muscles as well. You have to remember where the bombs were and guess where your opponent's men and other assets might be as you move across the field to capture the opponent's flag. Some of you might like the Battleship game as well. Both are great fun to play and build your focus, memory, and intuition.

CHAPTER SUMMARY

In this chapter, we have learned much about our inner self, intuition, and instinct, where these things come from and how they affect our daily lives. Scientists and spiritualists alike believe that we should all nurture and learn more about our intuition. It is usually set between instinct and logical thinking. Intuition is influenced by our life traumas and can be blocked by our negative thoughts and emotions. Intuition should always be used for the benefit of others.

Here the two camps diverge. Scientists cannot factually prove intuitive thoughts and feelings beyond a reasonable doubt but believe it exists and is fallible or sometimes unreliable. Spiritualists know that intuition is generally correct almost all of the time based on the information it has received and asked of it. It takes time, practice, and patience to allow your intuitive self to grow and get better at sending you messages to help you achieve your goals. Only when self-doubt comes creeping into our consciousness do we feel that our intuition may be wrong.

In the next chapter, you will learn all about spirit guides and how to connect with them.

8

CONNECT WITH YOUR SPIRIT GUIDES

THE DIFFERENCE BETWEEN THE HIGHER SELF AND SPIRIT GUIDES

Consider for a moment that there are different planes of existence. We are on this road of life working on our spiritual journey through lifetimes of living, studying, and learning. If you believe in these things, as you do with your empathic abilities, you have already started asking other energy beings to assist you. Whether you pray to a single deity or several, most souls believe that they have someone watching over them all through their lives. You can consider them guardian angels or spirit guides.

There is a difference between your family spirits protecting you and guiding you and an actual spirit guide. Spirit guides act as assigned teachers and helpers to your soul. You just have to learn how to introduce yourself to one or more of them and believe that they are there to help you achieve your aims in this life. The ultimate goal is always to progress to the next one. Essentially, they are advanced spirits who have learned all they have been assigned to learn on the earthly plane and are now helping other souls with their journey. They will only come when invited.

You have your ego, your higher self, and your spirit guide. Your ego just wants to protect you from anything harmful in your life. It keeps you from taking that leap into starting your own business, ending a non-productive relationship, or even jumping in the car to have some fun when there are so many chores to do at home. It is not a good or bad part of your being, just the part that doesn't like risks of any kind. It tells you "I can't" all the time.

Your higher self is your spiritual soul that generally pops in and out of your life when you are just doing repetitive chores. It is your mind wandering and thinking about your problems and possible solutions. It encourages you to take risks and explore creative ways to do things. It sounds like you but uses words like "we" and "you" instead of "I." The higher self is considered loving, supportive, and wise. *If we connect with our higher self on a daily basis, we begin developing a healthy habit of soothing our emotions and quieting our fears by listening to the wisdom of our higher self.* We do this by meditation and speaking directly to our higher selves. Self-love and self-talk habits can build self-confidence too.

LITTLE CHILDREN AND FAITH

Children reflect fun, purity, innocence, joy, playfulness, love, spirit, creativity, imagination, and truth—reminding us of what we "once" were.

We have all probably witnessed the sense of wonder in small children as they view the world. We may not remember our own trusting and believing state at such a young age, but most of us openly loved, believed, and enjoyed our everyday existence. For the most part, children start off thinking that anything and everything is possible. They are more open to the spirits and energies around us. They may have "imaginary" friends with whom they talk and play. Sadly, we all seem to lose that ability just so we can appear "normal" to our friends, family, teachers, and classmates.

Now that you are exploring your empathic abilities (whichever they may be) and would like to have help along your journey, you need to encourage your inner child to come back to the surface. No, not your childish behaviors, but your inner innocence and complete belief, love, and gratitude for living. You need to find your "JOY", as it were, and connect to your higher self and your spirit guides. Reawaken the magic and awe of breathing in and out, watch a brilliant sunrise or sunset, immerse yourself in the feeling of creating life in your garden, or just watch a hummingbird.

Some Tips for Helping Your Inner Child Resurface

Be spontaneous - let er' rip now and then just do it	*Loosen up* – don't be an old stick-in-the-mud
Play & Create – dance, party, craft, make sandcastles, swing on the swings	*Laugh Out Loud* – regularly and often, as it increases endorphins
Cancel Fear – Step into your fears and watch them dissolve	*Observe the roses* – as I said, watch the birds play and smile
Be affectionate – (within reason) – smile, hug, if appropriate, genuinely care* – it doesn't have to be returned*	*Listen to your intuition* – pay attention to what your heart and guts tell you
Use your imagination – dreaming can manifest into a pleasant reality*	Learn some fun kid jokes – it can' hurt

DIFFERENT TYPES OF SPIRIT GUIDES

Spirit guides are entities designed to help and advise you on this physical plane of existence. They are kindly entities, concerned explicitly for your well-being—nothing more.

Just as there are different kinds of people in the world, there are different kinds of spirit guides outside of it. They are spiritual energies you can tap into. In most cases, they are more of a teacher; they listen and guide you. They may project confidence, knowledge, and well-being. This study will talk about the four basic types of spirit guides that are generally attached to your particular soul.

The main one is like your best friend. He/she/it was assigned to you when you first landed on this earthly plane of existence. They are just here to help in the best way possible with almost everything that happens along your journey. But they must be invited in. Remember, they may not come right away or every single time. And they do tend to be more metaphorical in their messages.

The next type of spirit guide is what is considered a guardian guide. They are concerned for your physical and emotional well-being. A guardian guide will warn you about a dangerous situation (gut intuition, too), an unhealthy relationship or a toxic job situation. That fluttering, shivering feeling you get when you walk into a place is probably your guardian guide telling you to turn around and get the heck out of there.

The wisdom or scholar guide is the teacher. Yes, your best friend guide also wants to help you learn about your life, choices, and abilities, but the scholar guide is more of a specialist. For example, if you have to take a math test, a math scholar guide is ready to help you study and prepare for that test. Likewise, if you want to learn a language for an upcoming trip, you can call on a specialist guide to help you get the right resources and practice that particular skill.

The body-balance guides are only concerned with your health and well-being. They are the ones nagging you to eat right, get out there and exercise. Some are able to help you find the right doctor to assist you with a particular medical situation. A few may help you pick the right Yoga professional if you so choose. This type of thing is also considered a "specialty", but these guides can help you move in the right direction for you and your body.

Then there are some "all-purpose" or short-term guides. If you have some special circumstance or situation and are unsure which guide can help you, ask the universe for help. There are spirit guides assigned to every problem a human being will face. With a generic, universal appeal, you might be able to elicit the help of one of these guides. They are like the "handyman or woman" in the guide realm. Hey, you don't know until you ask.

HOW TO MEET YOUR SPIRIT GUIDE?

Meeting your spirit guide is like most things in life. First, you have to go where they are to meet the best in the field. If you want to meet baseball players, you go to baseball games. If you want to meet a good Yoga coach, you go down to your local gym and get some recommendations. If you want to meet the spirit guide(s) assigned to you, then you will have to introduce yourself on the "spiritual" back porch, so to speak, and acknowledge their existence. Next, you will need to meditate. Finally, be grateful for their help in everything you ask of them.

As with most learning experiences, you should grab a couple of pens and paper or your notebook to record your sessions each and every time. All good investigators should record their attempts, note their results, and analyze their outcomes. Each time you try will be another learning experience. Some things will work, and others may not. Only by recording everything you try will you learn if it's working or not. Then, as with all good practice, your meetings will be more productive each time. Below is a list of steps to try your first time out. You will do most of these things every time, but you might want to add another step later if you are not getting the results you hoped for.

- Find a peaceful place in your heart and mind and visit for a while.
- Empty your head and just breathe while sitting in the shower.
- Sit outside in the shade and watch the birds, butterflies, or dogs frolic and play.
- Imagine golden or even energy surrounding you in warmth.
- Create a quick list of five things you are grateful for at that moment.

"Spirit guide, I invite you into my space. I would like to establish an open, clear communication dialogue with you." This is a sample of what you might say to begin your session. The spirit guide may communicate in words, pictures, or just feelings. You must be clear in your requests and only ask about one or two things in each session.

Another example would be, *"Thank you, guides of the*

highest truth and compassion, for showing me what I need to know." No matter what you need assistance with, you might want to say something similar, only changing "I need to know" to what you want to know. Go into detail. Do not be afraid of being whimsical with your request. Remember the "child-like" wonder we hope to get back in our lives?

He/she/it is a spirit guide and only wants what is best for you. With a clear understanding of the help you need, they are more able to advise, get you some assistance, or provide what is necessary to accomplish the task. The responses may be hard to interpret. It could be repeated numbers or a picture in your mind that keeps showing up everywhere you look. Make a note of where you are and what is going on in those times. But you have to believe they will help you achieve your current goal. Let it go for now.

Side note: Just ask if you want to know the spirit guide's name. Whatever name pops into your head first will be the right one.

Once you are done with your session, the very first thing you should get in the habit of doing is recording what you saw, felt, and even smelled. Note down the entire experience in as much detail as you can remember. By keeping a record of your sessions, you are imprinting the experiences into your conscious mind. Then, when you receive the help you need, make sure to thank your guides. The more grateful you are for their support, the more help they will be able to give.

HOW TO CREATE A RELATIONSHIP WITH YOUR SPIRIT GUIDES

Creating a relationship with your spirit guide requires time, practice, and patience. It may involve a lot of writing as well. But, for some reason, the actual practice of writing stuff down on a piece of paper (journal or composition book) with a blue or black ink pen (pencils tend to fade and other ink colors do not last as long) helps you communicate better with the spiritual energy. It also helps reinforce what you are asking for and whether or not you receive it.

However, if you do not get that tricked-out monster truck your little heart is craving, you probably don't really need it. But asking for help in obtaining reliable and safe transportation is not beyond the realm of possibilities. Oh, better not go down that rabbit hole. Anyway, connecting to your spirit guides will take practice, an attitude of gratefulness, and the willingness to listen and do what needs to be done. After all, you are asking for help. Therefore, you have to do the work required to fulfill your own desires and goals.

Ask for assistance out loud	"Love and peace" is an empath's and a guide's preferred energy
Confirmation is nice – *"Ask for a sign"*	You may have to interpret what you receive and put it to use
Always be grateful for any assistance you receive with an *"open heart"*	You asked, now believe it will work, in its own time
Be "joyful" when you make contact—even your guides like a happy person.	Trust in yourself and your abilities. Confidence breeds confidence.

HOW DO I KNOW WHEN MY SPIRIT GUIDE IS CLOSE TO ME?

Your imagination and intuition come from the same part of your brain. If you imagine it to be so, it will manifest in one form or another. There are a few signs you can look for to intuit when your spirit guide is with you:

- Colored energy in and around your body
- A feeling of well-being
- Creative and random ideas or memories keep popping into your head
- Slight electric pulses coming from specific parts of your body

These are some examples of the feelings and sensations you might encounter when your spirit guides are with you. The best indicator might be your thoughts and feelings. After your sessions, check to see if you feel at peace. Since these guides have completed their earthly journey, they have gained the wisdom of the cosmos and only wish to see you succeed. A feeling of calm and peace and whatever image they want to project should be all that you sense each time. Remember to always approach each session with a sense of love, patience, and gratitude. The emotions you feel will be returned.

UNDERSTANDING YOUR DREAMS

The interpretation of dreams has been going on for millennia. Some believe them to be portents of things to come. Modern scientists of all kinds acknowledge that our unconscious mind converses with the conscious mind while we are sleeping. Mostly, it is trying to work out problems that you have encountered. Some say they are not necessary for our physical well-being; however, psychologists agree that they are necessary for our mental health.

Writers may go to sleep worrying about their plot. Their unconscious mind will walk through the different scenarios trying to finish or perfect the storyline so the author will have some brilliant prose to type up the next day. Accountants dream about numbers, and medical professionals will probably dream about procedures and patient illnesses. All this really says is that dreams are personal. They are unique to the individual. There may be some similarities in people's dreams. After all, we are all human and experience most of the same worries and concerns every day. But, they are, and should be, treated as unique to that person.

The best way to understand your dreams is to write them down every time you wake up. Having a dream journal and pen next to your bed will help you get in the habit of writing the things that you saw, felt, smelled, and heard during your dreaming state. Keeping a record of your dreams can help you learn more about yourself and how your unconscious mind tries to assist in problem-solving.

Some of you may say, "I do not dream" or "I just don't remember my dreams." Well, you do, and you can if you want to. Every morning when you wake up, write down what you recall. If you don't remember anything, then write that down as well. You are telling your conscious mind to let your unconscious remember what is going on. Pretty soon, you will be remembering what you dreamed about. That, too, takes a willingness to try, patience, and persistence.

Another great thing about writing down your dreams is that it helps you connect with your spirit guides. In our dreams, we are naturally relaxed and open to other energies. Before you go to bed, tell yourself that you are inviting the assigned spirit guide to help you with whatever problem you are having. Your breathing techniques will come into play here too. Do not forget to be grateful for their assistance and believe that they will help you achieve your goal. Then just relax and let it go.

Imagination is everything.
It is the preview of life's coming attractions.
Imagination is more important than knowledge.
Never give up on what you really want to do.
A person with big dreams is more powerful than
one with all the facts.

– Albert Einstein

SPIRIT GUIDES: HOW THEY USE OUR DREAMS

Dreaming is such a great way to get things done. You not only have dreams for your future, your family, your friends, and your work life, but your dreams will help you work out any problems during your body's downtime. *Spirit guide dreams carry important messages for our healing, growth, and alignment.* They help us discover a new purpose in life, help heal inner wounds, learn the next steps to achieving our work and life goals, and inspire us to make changes when necessary. You know you are having spirit-guided dreams if you notice that the dreams are repeated several times. There might be special characters that guide you through the dream. It may be someone you recognize but do not necessarily know in person. I personally would like to have Abraham Lincoln help me with my next big speech! Finally, the dreams may take on an ethereal quality. Not to sound too "whoo, whoo," but if you dream about a foggy place with light crystals or purple trees next to a pink stream with blue apples on the ground, you are probably with your spirit guide.

CHAPTER SUMMARY

In this chapter, we learned more about how meditation can help us in our psychic and regular daily lives. There is a difference between our "higher selves," our ego, and our "spirit guides." All of which are part of our learning experience in this life. Our higher self is us, only closer to the spiritual plane. It envelopes us in self-love, allows us to work out problems through self-talk, and only wants the best for us. It does tend to pop in and out without an invitation and usually when our mind is just wandering. The ego is the frightened child in us. It tells us we can't or shouldn't do things. It, too, only wants to protect us but mostly in negative ways. The spirit guide must be invited in to help us with our goals, our needs, and our learning about ourselves. And finally, we touched on the subject of our dreams. They help us work out problems and can be a great way to communicate with our spirit guides.

In the final chapter, we will discuss spiritual healing. Do you have spiritual healing capabilities? We will find out more about how to tell if you do and how to help that ability grow.

9

SIGNS YOU HAVE SPIRITUAL HEALING
CAPABILITIES

SELF-HEALING

You may have heard the phrase, "Physician heal thyself." It is a biblical proverb which means take care of your own problems first and not just those of others. We have a great capacity for taking care of ourselves if we can just get out of our own way. Our brain and body can help fix most things on their own. Unfortunately, life gets in the way and prevents us from taking care of our physical and mental well-being. The traumas we experience throughout our lifetime can pile up and hinder our ability to take care of ourselves. We have discussed ways to help ourselves become healthier, happier, well-adjusted humans and empaths throughout this book.

It all begins with learning how we can help resolve our own issues, let go of the past, encourage the universal beings to help us along the way, and create a routine of helpful self-healing and self-love

S.C . ROWSE I 126

techniques. Some of this comes from taking better care of ourselves by eating right, getting exercise, reducing life stresses, and having some fun every now and again. It includes learning to accept ourselves as we are, learning new things every day and practicing the gifts we have been given. There is nothing better for your soul than discovering your purpose, learning how to use your gifts, and helping others.

Mastering the ability to become healthy and keep yourself healthy and happy will spread to other areas of your life

1. *Change your meaning* – use audio-guided self-hypnosis to help change certain aspects of your personality, boost your confidence, establish good habits, and much more.
2. *Make the unfamiliar familiar* – through the judicious use of selected positive affirmations, you can help retrain your brain to focus on those activities and feelings that are beneficial to you and your well-being.
3. *Use visualization to heal yourself*–another rule is that you get more of whatever you focus on. Whatever you visualize can happen with time, patience, and persistence. Seeing yourself how you would like to be is the first step in achieving these goals.
4. *Try practicing regular meditation* –this can be the stepping stone to healing as well. Meditation is more than just relaxing techniques and

connecting to your spirit guides. You can use it to heal as well. (Chi - Natural Healing Energy)

Meditation allows you to take back control of your thoughts, feelings, and emotions by giving your mind space to reset and rejuvenate. Finding the time and space to do this several times a day, if necessary, can help clear out any excess stuff that may be clogging your intuitive self.

- Grab your favorite timing device (egg timers or even the timer on your phone will work).

- Find a comfortable seated position with space around you so that you will not fall down.

- Take a deep breath in through the nose and close your eyes.

- Breathe out slowly through the mouth.

- Concentrate on just your breathing and count.

- Should a stray thought appear, just acknowledge it but let it pass on through.

- When the timer goes off, stand up and shake out all your limbs.

Healing meditation is meant to consciously promote the health of the mind, body, and spirit. The main intention of healing meditation is to cultivate balance.

SPIRITUAL HEALING

Spiritual healing is natural, non-invasive and aims to bring the recipient into balance and a state of well-being on all levels.

You can use the techniques described above to heal yourself. Almost everyone has this ability to help themselves heal. Some use their spiritual energy to heal others. Others have studied and trained and have been helping heal mental and physical ailments for years. Recently, there have been several studies by physicians and other scientists to try and quantify this ability. They know it exists and have seen it work in their own practices and hospitals.

The problem is that spiritual healing is not an exact practice because the healer never knows if what they are there to heal is a physical ailment, mental anguish, or a combination of the two. Even with specific intentions and the patient's cooperation, the results are never really predictable enough for scientists to be able to prove their effectiveness. However, over the last several years, seeing the efficacy of remote healing, group prayer, and hands-on healers, physicians and educators are incorporating the patient's religious and spiritual preferences into their treatment plans. Even medical schools are developing courses for their students to learn more about this phenomenon. There are even spiritual healing centers located all around the world.

Scientists have been able to prove some of what happens when a spiritual healer works with their clients. Some people can perceive electro-magnetic fields during a healing, with the brain showing low-frequency activity. The electro-encephalograms demonstrated increased alpha brain waves in the healer and the patient synchronizing during the healing session. And this is now supported by quantum physics. *"It is considered that healing, through the input of thought at an energetic level, can influence the harmony of the mind, body, and spirit."*

Now you might ask, what qualities do these spiritual healers possess? I'm glad you asked:

- They may sometimes have a brain-centered disability like autism or dyslexia.
- They have a strong sense of the spiritual but are not necessarily religious.
- They feel connected to the "natural worlds," such as plants, animals, rivers and oceans.
- Animals like them, and they, in turn, love and protect them to a sometimes extreme degree.
- They are creative in a variety of ways, for example, sculpture, ceramics, painting, music, etc.
- They associate more closely with specific cultures or geographic regions.
- They sometimes have wide mood swings between wanting to be with people and needing lots of solitude.

This is by no means a comprehensive list, but it will give you some idea of the typical traits these healers might have. If you think you might want to learn to be a spiritual healer, there are training classes available at spiritual healing centers where you can get more information and the names of their healers who might be willing to talk to you. Of course, there is also a lot of information available on the internet. But getting in contact with a couple of spiritual healers yourself is always preferable to blindly following information you stumbled across on the web.

Components of spiritual healing

Universal energy can be directed by someone intentionally to help someone in pain, sickness, or suffering emotional distress. When the healer focuses on the patient's body, the aura or human energy field vibrates at a higher frequency. This can be likened to striking a tuning fork and then placing it on the body part in question. And in essence, the two bodies' energy merges for a moment while the healer releases the pain or repairs the psychic damage they see. This can improve the person's health and, with some repeated treatments, can continue to strengthen that person's body and mind. The patient will generally feel very little; hopefully just a lightening of spirit or release of pain and tension. You can never guarantee any health or mental healing for your patient. You can only convey your intentions to help, and with their cooperation, you can affect some change in their current situation.

Su Mason of the Royal College of Psychiatrists in the U.K., in his white paper entitled, "Spiritual Healing: What is it? Does it work and does it have a place in modern healthcare?" has a scripted exercise in his appendix. It is entitled "Visualization to Raise Energetic Vibrations." It is a little too long to add here but well worth the read.

He recommends doing this exercise regularly throughout your healing day as it is a powerful healing energy visualization technique.

SELF-HYPNOSIS TO HEAL

Self-hypnosis is very similar to meditation. Both involve entering a calm and relaxed state. The main difference is that you are working on a specific goal with self-hypnosis. *There is no particular goal in a typical meditation session, just an easy acceptance of wherever the mind goes without judgment or intention.* There are several techniques to begin teaching yourself self-hypnosis. You will want to start with the slower method. Once you have practiced and become comfortable with that approach, you can learn both the quicker and deeper techniques.

You will need a quiet place, no distractions for a minimum of 15 to 20 minutes each session, and unlike meditation, you really need an audio guide to help you through. You can pre-record your own session or use one of the many apps available. Then, set your timer and your intention (goal) for that session, and tell yourself you will awake refreshed and calm should you get interrupted. And, of course, when the timer goes off, take a deep breath in, let it out, and you will awake feeling refreshed and better than before. Each of these steps is needed to help you get into a self-hypnosis induced state. It is a suggestive state where your subconscious mind is being opened. You can now pay full attention to the suggestions you want to give yourself. Remember, only you can induce this type of state in your mind.

A couple of notes for the "intention or goal" part of the session:

Say it with conviction: You want the suggestion or goal to be stated in a firm but loving manner. You want this goal to work, so no guilt or being wishy-washy.

Phrase suggestions in the present tense: Say it as if it is already done. Fix it in your brain, and your mind will make it so.

Phrase your suggestion as a positive: Phrases that state what you want rather than what you do not want are more powerful.

Make suggestions realistic: The goal should be obtainable in a reasonable time. You will get discouraged with larger goals. Start small and build from there.

Repeat the suggestions: Keep repeating the positive, obtainable goal several times during the session. It usually takes the brain six or seven times to hear and see something for it to stick.

Using imagery and action: Most of us are visual learners. Use descriptive images and movement to emphasize your achieving your goal, what it will look like, and how you will feel – the more details, the better.

Each session should only last about ten to fifteen minutes but keep at it every day. Visualize attaining your goal all through the day as well. You will be reinforcing the learning sessions and helping your unconscious brain work on how to achieve your goal.

SAMPLE EXERCISES (SCRIPTS) TO USE IN SELF-HYPNOSIS

There are several ways to achieve your goals through self-hypnosis. You may need help creating the scripts for your audio sessions to help guide you through each one. If this kind of thing works for you, it would be nice to start with some tried-and-true dialogue. We have gathered informational resources to help you work on four areas of your life. These are established scripts just to get you started. You may have to add some preparatory steps to the beginning and a cool-down part at the end. DO write them all out first. Practice them prior to using your self-hypnosis routine, and, with time and repetition, you will be able to create your own dialogues for any given situation.

Below are some complete scripts; others will need a beginning and end to be a complete session. With time and practice, you will be able to create your own texts for any given situation.

Eliminate Self-Sabotage

We all have problems with being a little self-destructive in our daily lives. This is highly detrimental to our well-being, our relationship with others, and even our future selves. I recommend the book by Rene A. Bastarache published in 2009, called *"The Everything Hypnosis Book: Learn to Use Your Mental Power to Take Control of Your Life"*. There is a lot of helpful information on self-hypnosis, including several useful scripts to get you started. Record them. Use Them. And eventually, you can write your own that will fit your specific needs.

Inside, you will find several scripts you can record for yourself to use on a regular basis in your self-hypnosis sessions. Reading, learning, and practicing new skills is how we all grow, even psychics.

Try the following dialogue during your next self-hypnosis session:

You are now highly motivated. You exude confidence in all that you do.

Self-doubt and fear are things of the past, and you now replace them with confidence and conviction. You trust your abilities and know that you can do anything you set your mind on. You are successful in all that you do. Other people enjoy being around you because of your confidence and ability. You have a very open mind and are creative.

You are your own best friend and can accomplish anything you wish.

You are a self-confident, successful winner who accomplishes your goals.

Your only limitation is your imagination, and now you let your imagination run free. You are a winner, and your life is a series of successes.

You allow only positive thoughts to run through your mind. You have a strong drive to be successful, to be a winner. You are confident and follow through with any task that you take on. You finish all tasks in a positive manner and never have any doubt that you will succeed.

Your new motto is, Do it now! You will find that you are success-oriented, starting right now. You expect to succeed in everything.

You feel enthusiasm and confidence in all that you do.

From now on, you no longer procrastinate. You feel a sense of urgency to complete everything that needs to be done. You feel a sense of satisfaction as you accomplish more and more each day. Every day your work gets easier to achieve, to finish.

You are going to become a doer rather than a worrier. You know that you will do your best, and your best will become better and better.

You'll do it now! By leaving procrastination behind, you will find that you have more time to do the things that you enjoy. You'll become more organized, more in control, and more confident. You'll find that your free time is indeed just that, free time!

Stress Reduction Script

There are many ways to reduce stress, and we have covered quite a few of them already. Just the practice of meditation can relieve a lot of your everyday stress, like getting enough exercise, sleep, and doing something just for fun.

As with each of these self-hypnosis sessions, you will be concentrating on your breathing, saying positive affirmations, and visualizing those positive forces that will assist you with your everyday life's challenges.

If you have an unusual amount of stress, try the following:

Read this script directly into your recorder as it will

be a whole self-contained session

Take a deep breath ... and hold it for a few seconds ... exhale and relax ... Now take a second deep breath, as deep as you can ... and as you exhale just let go of any stress... Take a third deep breath ...as deep as you can ... hold it ... and exhale ... just think the words "relax now."

This is your new solution for stress ... Whenever you become stressed in the future ... you'll simply relax ... take three deep breaths ... and on your third one, as you exhale ... you will simply say to yourself the words relax now.

You are now developing a new way to relax ... you are letting go of the stress of the past ... You wish to no longer have depression or anger in your life ... So from now on, you choose to be relaxed ... You choose to be calm ... and you choose to be in control in all that you do ... because your health is important to you ... You are changing the way that you used to act. You are replacing it with the new, positive suggestions I am about to give you ... By following these few simple suggestions ... you'll find yourself being stress-free in all that you do ... You'll find yourself being relaxed in situations you may not have previously been relaxed in .... With your new relaxed lifestyle ... you'll find yourself being happier ... more positive ... and enjoying everything you do.

The first suggestion is that whenever you find yourself having negative, unproductive thoughts, you'll immediately say the word STOP! ... Let me repeat that to you, so it is perfectly clear ... Whenever you find yourself having negative, unproductive thoughts, you'll immediately say the word STOP! ... and as soon as you say the word STOP! ... you'll find that the negative thoughts you were having just disappear ... You will be able to start a new, positive thought process.

The following technique is the art of accepting things as they are rather than allowing them to escalate out of control ... From this moment on ... anytime you find yourself getting stressed because of a situation that seems to be going out of control ... You will stop worrying about what could happen ... all the negative scenarios ... and instead ... you will accept ... what has happened precisely for what it is ... You can use your thought processes to think the situation through to see what reasonable outcomes there may be ... realizing that once you have worked through them, they are always better than if you had let your mind run wild and worried ... Worry is a thing of the past ... it is now replaced ... with relaxation.

You are now in control ... of your thoughts ... your feelings ... and your emotions ... you have become someone who acts ... rather than reacts ... which simply means that in any given situation ... you ... and only you ... choose ... how you are going to respond ... or to behave ... and now you choose to act ... calmly ... positively ... and in control.

Just for a moment, I would like you to concentrate on your breathing ... take a breath in ... and exhale, and as soon as you feel all the breath leave your body and you are prepared to take another breath, quietly count to twenty-five ... take a second breath, not necessarily a deep one, just a normal one, and exhale ... and when that breath is finished, count under your breath to twenty-four ... then take another normal breath, whatever length seems comfortable to you ... and exhale ... then count, twenty-three ... and continue doing this on your own, with another breath, counting twenty-two, and twenty-one, all the way down to one ... and as soon as you take your last deep breath, exhale, and say the number one, you will open your eyes ... feeling calm ... and relaxed ... in every way ... in fact, you will find yourself more relaxed than you have ever been before.

So continue counting even as I speak ... each one of your breaths ... concentrating on your breathing ... noticing the flow of the air ... as it enters your body ... fills you up ... and then leaves once again ... study the sensations you feel ... with every breath you take, you relax more and more, with every breath you take, you feel more peaceful and more serene as you go down deeper and deeper into the relaxed state ... and as soon as you count to the number one, you will open your eyes once again feeling wonderful in every way.

Enjoying Life Script

Remember that only you can decide how you will live this life and how you will go about finding ways to enjoy it. What does a joyous life look like to you? It is more of a positive self-talk speech to make you aware of your choices in this life. You deserve to be happy, and there are still many lessons to learn before you are through. Writing these "pep talks" out in long form and recording them for yourself will assist you in learning how to move forward in your journey and enjoy the happiness you find along the way. And, if you help someone else, that would be a bonus.

Once you have decided on those goals, then try out this script:

Happiness occurs in the present. The past is gone, and the future has not arrived yet.

Happiness is all that you have. Keep in mind that enjoying life is a choice. You can choose to be happy, or you can choose to be sad. You choose to be happy. You choose to enjoy each moment of your life.

From this moment on, find new ways to enjoy your life. Even throughout the routine of your day, you can enjoy your life more than ever before if you choose to. All you need to do is break down each portion of your day, whether routine or not, and ask yourself how you can make that part of your day better.

Take a moment right now and imagine the rest of this day. What will you be doing immediately after the end of this session?

Whatever it is, what can you do to make it better? Consider that question seriously. How can you make it better? Even if it is a simple task like going to the grocery store, what can you do differently to make it more enjoyable?

Perhaps you can play your favorite music while you are driving there. Maybe, you can run and feel energized by the exercise rather than walking to your vehicle. At the grocery store, buy something special just to treat yourself. Greet the cashier with an extra warm smile, and show genuine concern for her well-being. You may even take the opportunity to help someone struggling with a large package or purchase.

One of the greatest ways to feel happier is to be of service to others. Being of service to others enhances your own life. Making someone else happy makes you happy. By helping someone, you are helping yourself. Take the time to think of how you can brighten up someone else's day, whether through a simple compliment or helping someone somehow.

Make it a habit to improve the various parts of your day, even the mundane sections, and you will find that you will enjoy life more than you could have ever dreamed. Enjoy your life ... enjoy being happy. You have a right to be happy and enjoy everything you do.

Healing with White Light

There are as many different healing scripts as there are ailments. Generally, you want to personalize your dialogue to the particular condition you wish to fix, change, or just get some relief from. There is one for the healers as well. It is another visualization technique called "The Healing White Light." Again, read the script into a recorder and play it through as you go through your self-hypnosis routine. It is well worth the read, and as empaths, we need all the "white light" assistance we can get. You can, of course, change the script if you like, using different words, feelings, and affirmations to make it more personal to you and your situation. Don't be afraid to experiment. These scripts should all resonate with you and help you fulfill your destiny.

This is a visualized Healing with White Light Script

Imagine a healing white light just above your head. This is a light that heals completely or eases all your pain. The light will act similarly to a scanner from a photocopier. As the light descends over your head, scanning your face, the pain will recede from the area the light passes over. You will feel wonderful. It then continue to scan lower and lower until it scans your entire body and all the pain is gone.

You can also imagine that you are filled with a healing white light. As you survey your entire body, see if you can find where there might be leaks, and the light is escaping. Those areas need to be healed, and you should mentally imagine yourself fixing those leaks. Plug them up, so the light is contained within you. Fixing these leaks will lessen your pain.

I want you to use your imagination. Take a deep breath and hold it for a second; as you breathe in, imagine yourself breathing in pure energy from the universe. You can even visualize this energy as a bright, white, healing, fluffy substance. Each time you exhale, you release negativity and discomfort. Each time you inhale, you inhale more of that pure white energy until it fills you up completely. Imagine that the energy remains with you until it fills you completely.

Now mentally scan your entire body to see if you have any energy leaks. As you do, if you notice any leaks, you will see the white, comfortable energy visibly escaping. If you see any of these leaks, use your imagination and imagine yourself repairing them. Imagine it, and it will happen until the leaks are all repaired (pause a few moments).

Now that you have entirely repaired any leaks, you can allow the energy to continue to flow through you. As you inhale and exhale, the energy both enters and flows outwards, continually keeping you energized and feeling wonderful. As you continue to imagine this energy flowing in and out and filling you up, it seems to absorb itself into every cell of your being. It fills you up so much that it appears to form a protective shield around your body. This protective shield protects you from any negativity. No longer can the influence of anyone or anything drain your energy away.

AFFIRMATIONS FOR EVERY SITUATION

Affirmations, proclamations, and positive statements are all basically the same thing. We want to conquer our constant bad decision-making in life: you know, self-sabotaging our existence with negative energy, thoughts, and emotions. By writing down positive declarative statements and repeating them over and over, we instill their messages into our very being. We have all had negative ideas, images, words, etc., thrown at us all of our lives. They get ingrained into our psyche until we root them out and change them to a positive. Affirmations can be both negative and positive. But they must be as positive as possible for us to change. *A little note here, though: positive affirmations have adverse effects on those with low self-esteem. So please work on that first.*

They do work particularly well when you pair them with visualizations. That is probably why you see so many supporting messages pop up on your social media feeds with pretty scenes or even funny animals in the background. They get people's attention and are more easily remembered. Visualize your personal affirmations as well. You need to see yourself being that better person, obtaining that desired result, and meeting those expectations when you say the words.

LOFTY QUESTIONS TECHNIQUE

Before we begin with the affirmations exercises and techniques, let's look at "Lofty Questions" first. Lofty questions can also help you create your own effective affirmations. Once you have mastered this type of question, they will allow your subconscious mind and the universe to guide you towards a new and positive future. So, when you feel that an affirmation doesn't work, transform it into a lofty question.

The four rules to asking lofty questions

Phrase the question in the positive—you want

the question to have a positive spin. After all, we want the universe and our brains to show us positive things in our lives.

Start with the word "Why?"—starting with a "why" tells the brain we need to know something and opens the way for the subconscious to work on the answers.

Include the word "always" or "at all times"—this eliminates the chance of the issue not always being true or only happening sometimes. We would all prefer things that work each and every time.

Relaxed meditative state — your mind and body need to be ready to explore and accept the answers you are seeking before you start. No one can learn much of anything unless they are in a relaxed state.

Now for the hard part. That's right. It is time for you to create some "lofty questions" of your own. So, get out the old pen and paper, and remember the four rules above. Below are a couple of examples to get you started. Try these out for a few days, and then get into the habit of creating your own. They should be personal to you and your situation. You will need to repeat them often to get your mind and the universe working on them.

Why am I surrounded by beauty and creation?	Why am I always so good at bringing in enough money to pay all my bills, put it into savings, and have some left for fun too?
Why am I always so good at attracting enlightened friends?	Why do my readers always enjoy my writing?
Why does the universe always help me travel where I want?	Why do my dreams work out in the most exciting ways?

How to Write an Affirmation Statement

Think about the areas of your life that you'd like to change – It is much easier if you begin by writing these down in your journal. Use any layout style that suits you: grid style or one page per goal.

Turn negatives into positives – If you want to change something, make sure you assert it in a positive manner. We want to break a negative habit as quickly as possible. There is just too much negativity in the world already.

Be sure that your affirmation is credible and achievable – This is another area where you want to start small or in smaller chunks and then move forward to more demanding or challenging goals. For example, instead of picturing yourself in a size two pair of jeans, just try eating healthier and getting more exercise.

Write your affirmation in the present tense – You want your mind to see it happening now.

Say it with feeling – You have to believe it to make it

come true. The change will only happen if you are committed to it.

HEALING AFFIRMATIONS

When we create positive and healing statements, we release all the negative energy surrounding us, preventing us from moving forward. You can talk yourself into being sick without really trying. It is therefore also possible to convince yourself that you are getting healthier every day. With repetition and belief and the normal healthy activities of exercise, diet, meditation, and fun pastimes, you can keep your mind and body as fit as possible. "Neuroscience has proven that reciting affirmations can literally change the structure and general functionality of the brain" - quoted from an article written by Sarah Kristenson called "45 Healing Affirmations For your Mind, Body and Soul."

Below we have collected some positive affirmations for healing that you might want to use in your everyday routine. Some will resonate with you, and others may not. You can always create your own.

Healing Affirmations for the Mind

I am working to heal my health.

I will replace all negative energy with positive.

I am exercising to improve my mental health.

I love myself as myself and no one else.

I deserve to be loved as I am.

Healing Affirmations for the Body

I will eat lovely fruits and veggies every day.

My body deserves to move.

I am blessed to be in good health.

I am in love with my hair as it is.

I do not need approval from my peers for anything.

Healing Affirmations for the Soul

I am a walking, talking miracle of life.

I am at peace with my past and hopeful for my future.

I have everything I need for right now.

I will be in nature every day.

The universe will always work for me.

If you cannot find any affirmations that resonate with you or in your life at this point in time, why not think about some of the lofty questions we've already mentioned? Take some time, create your own, write them out or print them up, and post them around your home and work areas. Once you set your mind to it, you will create lofty questions and positive affirmations for yourself, your family and friends, and those you wish to help.

CHAPTER SUMMARY

We have reached the end of this chapter and have learned much about healing our minds and bodies through various techniques, including self-hypnosis, meditation, visualization, and affirmations. They each play a role in our daily lives as humans and empaths. We learned about spiritual healing and how to become an actual spiritual healer. There is probably much more to learn about these subjects and the ones in the previous chapters. We hope that the sample scripts and affirmations we have provided will help you reach your goals, enjoy your life, and help others along on their journey. These are being provided as a guide only. You will need to create your own based on your own needs and lifestyle.

LEAVE A REVIEW

We would be incredibly thankful if you could take just 60 seconds to write a brief review on Amazon, even if it's just a few sentences!

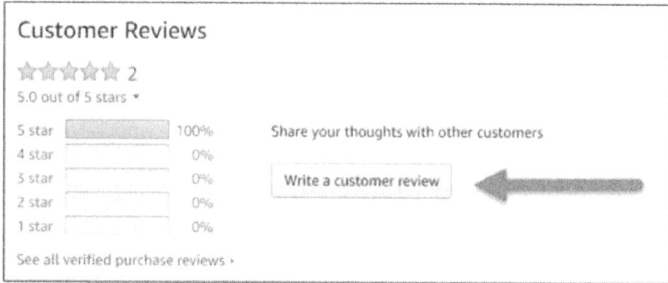

Scan the QR code below, leave your opinion and help another empath to make an informed decision!

Remember!

We are working together in changing the world, even if this means helping one empath at a time!

CONCLUSION

"Live life to the fullest. You have to color outside the lines once in a while if you want to make your life a masterpiece. Laugh some every day. Keep growing, keep dreaming, and keep following your heart. The important thing is not to stop questioning."

- Albert Einstein

We have come to the end of our journey for this book. There is a lot of information covered in a relatively short amount of time. We encourage you to read through some of the reference material if you have any more questions about any section. Investigating for yourself is a great way to begin your empathic education journey. There is so much not yet proven about these abilities, but they are real. You are blessed with a gift, and we hope you realize it.

As with any gift, there are responsibilities too. You need to learn your craft, practice every day, and seek guidance from fellow practitioners. And with anything in life, if there is a way to exploit something or someone, there will be people ready to do it. So, please protect yourself by embracing your talents, loving yourself, and learning how to get assistance from your spirit guides. Develop those resources to help others as you learn how to help yourself mentally and physically. Good luck with your journey.

References Pages

This book includes reference links that provide additional information, context, and credibility to the content. They demonstrate thorough research and allow you to delve deeper into the topics discussed, verify sources cited, and access related materials.

Scan the QR code using your smartphone or tablet to access them.

Printed in Great Britain
by Amazon

44365318R00086